The Happy [

Quick & Easy Homemade Dog Food Recipes That Meet AAFCO Standards for a Healthier, Happier Dog in Just 20 Minutes a Day!

Emma Taylor

As a special thank-you, I have prepared three exclusive bonuses to help you continue your journey toward better canine nutrition! 🐾

▦ Simply scan the QR code at the end of the book to access your gifts!

Disclaimer

This book has been carefully crafted using information sourced from professional canine nutrition books, scientific articles, and reputable pet health resources. While every effort has been made to ensure accuracy and provide valuable insights into homemade dog nutrition, this book was not written by a veterinarian or certified pet nutritionist.

Every dog is unique, and their dietary needs can vary based on breed, age, health conditions, and lifestyle. Before making any significant changes to your dog's diet, it is always recommended to consult with a trusted veterinarian or a certified canine nutritionist. They can provide personalized guidance and ensure that your homemade meals meet your dog's specific nutritional requirements.

The recipes and recommendations in this book are intended as a general resource for pet owners who want to prepare nutritious, balanced meals at home. They should not replace professional veterinary advice, diagnosis, or treatment. If you have any concerns about your dog's health, allergies, or special dietary needs, please seek guidance from a qualified professional.

By using this book, you acknowledge that you are responsible for your dog's diet and well-being. Thank you for being a dedicated and caring pet owner!

Contents

Introduction

If you're reading this book, chances are you want to provide the very best for your dog—because after all, our furry companions aren't just pets, they're family. Just like us, dogs thrive on fresh, nutritious food, and *what better way to ensure their health and happiness than by preparing their meals at home?*

Homemade dog food is more than just a trend; it's a way to **take control of your dog's diet**, avoid unnecessary additives, and tailor meals to their unique needs. Whether you have a **playful puppy**, an **active adult**, or a **wise senior dog**, providing balanced, wholesome meals can help them live a longer, healthier, and more vibrant life.

But let's be honest—knowing what to feed your dog and how to prepare it can feel overwhelming at first. That's where this book comes in! This guide is designed to **help you navigate homemade dog food with confidence**, whether you're just starting out or looking to fine-tune your pup's nutrition.

We'll break down the basics of canine nutrition, covering essential nutrients, portion sizes, and meal prep strategies. You'll find recipes tailored for different life stages, dietary needs, and even tasty homemade treats for training and special occasions. Plus, we'll explore how to transition your dog from commercial food to homemade meals in a safe and stress-free way.

Feeding your dog fresh, home-cooked meals is an act of love, and it doesn't have to be complicated. With a little planning and the right information, you can make mealtime a nourishing and enjoyable experience for your beloved pup.

So, grab your apron, stock up on fresh ingredients, and let's embark on this rewarding journey together. **Your dog will thank you with wagging tails, bright eyes, and boundless energy!**

Emma

Chapter 1: The Basics of Dog Nutrition

Making homemade dog food reflects your love and dedication to your dog's health and happiness and is a wonderful choice that can greatly boost your dog's health, happiness, and overall well-being.

To ensure a smooth transition to this new diet, it's essential to **approach the change gradually to prevent digestive upset**. Start by mixing a small amount of the homemade food with their current food, gradually increasing the homemade portion over the course of a week or more, depending on how well your dog adapts. This slow transition allows your dog's digestive system to adjust and gives you the opportunity to monitor their reaction to the new diet, including any changes in energy levels, coat health, and overall demeanor.

Regular check-ups with a veterinarian ensure that your homemade dog food meets your dog's nutritional needs. It's vital to observe your dog's energy levels, weight, and overall health. Any notable changes might indicate the need to adjust their diet.

Understanding the basic principles of canine nutrition is crucial during this transition. Dogs, much like humans, thrive on a well-rounded diet that includes proteins, fats, carbohydrates, vitamins, minerals, and water in specific proportions. Let's dive deeper into each one of these components.

Proteins

Proteins are often referred to as the building blocks of life, and for good reason—they are essential for your dog's growth, repair, and overall well-being. Proteins are responsible for building and maintaining strong muscles, repairing tissues, supporting the immune system, and facilitating numerous enzymatic and hormonal processes in the body. This makes them a cornerstone of your dog's diet, no matter their age, breed, or activity level.

When selecting protein sources for your dog, quality is just as important as quantity. High-quality proteins are those that are easily digestible and packed with essential amino acids—the components your dog's body cannot produce on its own. Common and nutritious options include chicken, beef, turkey, and fish, but each comes with its own unique benefits that make it a valuable part of your dog's diet.

- 🐾 **Chicken** is a lean protein that is gentle on the stomach, making it an excellent choice for dogs with sensitivities or digestive issues. It's rich in essential amino acids, low in fat, and highly digestible, ensuring your dog can extract the maximum benefit from every bite.
- 🐾 **Beef**, on the other hand, is a powerhouse of nutrients, offering not just protein but also high levels of iron and zinc. Iron is vital for the production of healthy red blood cells and energy, while zinc supports a robust immune system and promotes healthy skin. Beef also provides a hearty, satisfying flavor that many dogs love.
- 🐾 **Turkey** is another fantastic option, particularly for dogs needing a low-fat diet. It provides a similar nutritional profile to chicken, with the added benefit of being slightly less likely to trigger food sensitivities or allergies in some dogs. Turkey is also rich in selenium, which plays a key role in maintaining metabolic health and supporting the immune system.
- 🐾 **Fish**, particularly oily varieties like salmon, trout, or sardines, adds a whole new dimension to your dog's diet. In addition to high-quality protein, fish is an excellent source of omega-3 fatty acids, which are renowned for their anti-inflammatory properties. These healthy fats support joint health, brain function, and a shiny, healthy coat, making fish a particularly valuable addition for aging dogs or those with skin conditions.

For variety, you might also consider **eggs**, which are highly digestible and provide an excellent mix of protein, vitamins, and minerals, including biotin, which promotes healthy skin and coat. **Lamb** is another option, often chosen for its rich flavor and suitability for dogs with specific protein allergies.

Fats

Fats are a vital component of your dog's diet, providing much more than just a source of energy. They play a key role in maintaining overall health and vitality by supporting cellular function, protecting vital organs, and aiding in the absorption of fat-soluble vitamins such as A, D, E, and K. These vitamins are essential for processes ranging from bone development to immune function, making fats an indispensable part of a balanced diet.

One of the most important roles of fats is their **contribution to a healthy coat and skin**. Dogs with a diet that includes high-quality fats often exhibit shiny coats and hydrated, supple skin, which are not just cosmetic benefits but also signs of underlying health. Additionally, fats provide insulation and help regulate body temperature, which is particularly important for active or outdoor dogs exposed to varying climates.

Healthy Sources of Fats

Incorporating high-quality fat sources into your dog's meals can have transformative benefits for their health.

Fish oil, for example, is an excellent source of omega-3 fatty acids, which have powerful anti-inflammatory properties. These fats are particularly beneficial for dogs with joint issues, such as arthritis, and can also promote cognitive function, making them a great addition for senior dogs. Fish oils derived from salmon, mackerel, or sardines are especially rich in DHA (docosahexaenoic acid) and EPA (eicosapentaenoic acid), two types of omega-3s known for their health-boosting effects.

Flaxseed oil is another valuable fat source, offering a plant-based alternative rich in alpha-linolenic acid (ALA), a precursor to omega-3 fatty acids. While dogs convert ALA to DHA and EPA less efficiently than humans, flaxseed oil remains a good choice for dogs with fish allergies or for those on a plant-based diet.

Other beneficial fat sources include **coconut oil**, which contains medium-chain triglycerides (MCTs) known for providing quick energy and supporting brain health, and **chicken fat**, which is a flavorful, easily digestible option that's often used in high-quality commercial dog foods.

The Role of Fats in Cognitive and Joint Health

Beyond the physical benefits, fats are crucial for maintaining cognitive health, especially in puppies and aging dogs. Omega-3 fatty acids are integral to brain development in young dogs and have been shown to slow cognitive decline in senior dogs. Similarly, these healthy fats can alleviate stiffness and discomfort in joints, making them a key dietary component for dogs prone to arthritis or other mobility issues.

Striking the Right Balance

While fats are essential, it's important to offer them in moderation. **Too much fat in a dog's diet can lead to obesity, pancreatitis, or other health problems**. The amount and type of fats your dog needs will depend on their age, breed, activity level, and overall health. For example, highly active dogs, such as working breeds, require more dietary fats to fuel their energy-intensive lifestyles, while less active dogs may benefit from a lower-fat diet to maintain a healthy weight.

When preparing homemade meals, it's also critical to balance fats with proteins and carbohydrates. Over-reliance on fats for calories can crowd out other essential nutrients, leading to an imbalanced diet. A good rule of thumb is to **include fats from diverse sources** while ensuring the total fat content remains within the recommended range for your dog's size and life stage.

Carbohydrates

Carbohydrates, though not a dog's primary energy source like proteins and fats, play a valuable and multifaceted role in their overall health. Carbs provide readily available energy, supply essential dietary fiber, and contribute vital vitamins and minerals that support a well-rounded diet. While dogs are classified as omnivores and can thrive on a range of diets, including carbohydrates in their meals can offer significant benefits for digestion, energy regulation, and overall well-being.

The Role of Carbohydrates

Carbohydrates break down into glucose, which is used by the body for energy. While dogs primarily rely on fats and proteins for fuel, carbs serve as a supplementary **energy source**, particularly for active or working dogs that burn a lot of calories. Beyond energy, carbohydrates **provide dietary fiber**, which is critical for maintaining healthy digestion and gut function. Fiber helps regulate bowel movements, prevents constipation, and fosters a healthy gut microbiome, which is linked to better immune function and overall health.

High-Quality Carbohydrate Sources

Not all carbohydrates are created equal, so selecting nutrient-dense and easily digestible sources is crucial for your dog's diet.

Whole grains like **brown rice, oats, quinoa, and barley** are excellent options, providing complex carbohydrates that release energy gradually, helping maintain steady energy levels. These grains also supply important nutrients such as B vitamins, iron, and magnesium. For dogs with sensitivities to gluten, rice and oats are particularly gentle and effective alternatives.

Starchy vegetables like **sweet potatoes, pumpkin, and squash** offer another rich source of complex carbohydrates and dietary fiber. These vegetables are packed with vitamins A and C, which support immune health and vision. **Sweet potatoes**, known for their natural sweetness, are a favorite due to their high antioxidant content.

Similarly, **legumes** such as **peas, lentils, and chickpeas** provide both energy and protein, contributing to muscle health while their fiber content aids digestion and promotes a feeling of fullness. Root vegetables like carrots and beets round out the selection, providing carbohydrates along with valuable nutrients like beta-carotene and antioxidants. These can be served raw, grated, or finely chopped for a crunchy treat, or cooked to enhance digestibility.

Fiber's Impact on Digestive Health

Fiber is one of the most significant contributions carbohydrates make to a dog's diet, playing a critical role in digestive health. Soluble fiber, found in foods like oats and barley, absorbs water to form a gel-like substance in the digestive tract, slowing digestion and helping regulate blood sugar levels. This can be particularly beneficial for dogs prone to diabetes. Insoluble fiber, present in whole grains, vegetables, and fruit peels, adds bulk to the stool and supports regular bowel movements, preventing issues like constipation or diarrhea. Including a balance of both soluble and insoluble fibers ensures optimal gut health and supports the absorption of nutrients.

In addition to digestive benefits, carbohydrates, particularly those high in fiber, contribute to satiety and can be helpful for dogs on a weight management plan. Foods like pumpkin and sweet potatoes are especially effective in this regard, providing a low-calorie way to add bulk to meals. This sense of fullness reduces overeating and supports healthy weight loss or maintenance.

Balancing Carbohydrates in Your Dog's Diet

Unlike humans, dogs require fewer carbs, so they should complement proteins and fats rather than dominate meals. Cooking grains and starchy vegetables enhances their digestibility, making them more suitable for your dog. Simple carbohydrates like white bread, sugary snacks, and processed grains should be avoided, as they offer little nutritional value and can lead to blood sugar spikes or weight gain. Monitor your dog's reactions to different carbs, as some may cause sensitivities, and adjust their diet accordingly by substituting with gentler options like sweet potatoes or peas.

Incorporating carbohydrates into your dog's meals doesn't have to be complicated. You might mix cooked brown rice or quinoa with lean protein or add a scoop of mashed sweet potatoes to their food. Homemade treats using ingredients like oats, pumpkin, or carrots can also be a great way to provide nutritious and satisfying snacks.

When chosen thoughtfully and served in appropriate amounts, carbohydrates enhance your dog's diet by providing energy, supporting digestive health, and adding variety to their meals.

But there is another aspect that is as important as feeding your dog the right macronutrients: make sure its hydration is on point. This is what chapter 2 is all about.

The table summarizes the main sources of the different macronutrients.

Macronutrient	Sources
Proteins	Chicken, beef, turkey, fish, eggs, lamb
Fat	Fish oil, flaxseed oil, coconut oil, chicken fat
Carbohydrates	Brown rice, oats, quinoa, barley, sweet potatoes, pumpkin, squash, peas, lentils, chickpeas

Chapter 2: Hydration

Proper hydration is just as critical as a balanced diet when it comes to your dog's health. Water is the foundation of all biological functions in your dog's body, supporting vital processes like digestion, nutrient absorption, and the elimination of waste. It also helps regulate body temperature, ensuring your dog stays cool in warm weather or after exercise, and contributes to healthy skin and a shiny coat. Without adequate hydration, these essential systems can become strained, potentially leading to health issues.

The amount of water your dog needs each day depends on several factors, including their size, activity level, diet, age, and the environment. A general guideline suggests that dogs need **approximately one ounce of water per pound of body weight daily**. For instance, a 50-pound dog would require at least 50 ounces of water. However, this baseline can increase significantly under certain conditions. If your dog primarily eats dry kibble, which contains little moisture compared to wet food or homemade meals, they'll need more water to compensate. Similarly, active dogs—whether they're participating in intense exercise, long walks, or are working breeds with demanding roles—will need extra hydration to replace fluids lost through panting and activity. Environmental factors also play a role; hot, humid weather or heated indoor environments can increase water loss, requiring your dog to drink more to stay hydrated.

For dogs that are reluctant to drink water, maintaining proper hydration can be a challenge. Fortunately, there are simple and effective strategies to encourage better water intake. Ensuring that water is always fresh and easily accessible is a key starting point. Dogs are more likely to drink if their water bowl is clean and filled with cool, fresh water, so changing it at least once a day is essential. Having multiple water bowls in different locations around your home can also make it more convenient for your dog to drink whenever they feel the need.

Incorporating more moisture into your dog's diet is another excellent way to boost hydration. Wet food or homemade dog food naturally contains more water than kibble, helping to meet your dog's fluid needs as they eat. If your dog's diet is primarily dry food, you can mix in a little water or low-sodium broth to make the kibble more hydrating and appealing.

Adding flavor to water can make it more enticing for dogs that are picky drinkers. A small splash of unsalted chicken or beef broth can encourage them to drink more, but it's important to ensure the broth is free from harmful ingredients like onions or excessive salt. Another fun and easy way to keep your dog hydrated is by offering ice cubes as a treat. Many dogs enjoy crunching on ice cubes or playing with them in their water bowl, especially on warm days. You can even freeze broth into ice cubes for an extra burst of flavor that doubles as hydration.

Observing your dog's drinking habits and adjusting their hydration strategies as needed is essential. Dogs that aren't drinking enough water may show signs like lethargy, dry gums, sunken eyes, or concentrated, dark urine. In such cases, it's vital to address the issue promptly to prevent dehydration, which can lead to serious health problems such as kidney issues or heatstroke in extreme cases.

Encouraging good hydration habits not only supports your dog's immediate health but also contributes to their long-term well-being. Whether through fresh water, moisture-rich foods, or creative solutions like flavored water or ice cubes, ensuring your dog stays properly hydrated will help them lead a vibrant, active, and healthy life.

Hydration During Exercise

Exercise is an important part of a dog's physical and mental health, but it also places additional demands on their hydration levels, especially for active dogs or those exercising in warm weather. **Proper hydration during physical activity is crucial for maintaining energy, preventing overheating, and supporting overall well-being.**

When dogs engage in vigorous activity, whether it's a long walk, a hike, a play session at the park, or training exercises, they lose water through panting and, to a lesser extent, through their paws. In hot or humid weather, this water loss increases significantly, putting them at risk of dehydration or even heatstroke if not addressed promptly. Providing your dog with access to water during exercise is essential to prevent these issues and to keep their body functioning optimally.

Carrying water for your dog on walks or outdoor activities should become a habit, particularly during warmer months. Collapsible water bowls, portable dog water bottles, or travel-friendly hydration packs are convenient options that make it easy to offer water wherever you go. While you're out, monitor your dog's behavior closely. Signs such as excessive panting, slowing down, or seeking shade may indicate that they need a water break. **Offering water at regular intervals**—every 15 to 30 minutes during extended activity—is a good rule of thumb, but it's also important to consider your dog's individual needs. Larger breeds, brachycephalic (flat-faced) breeds, and dogs with thick coats often require more frequent hydration.

When offering water, it's best to let your dog **sip small amounts at a time** rather than gulping down large quantities. Drinking too much water too quickly can lead to discomfort or, in rare cases, bloat—a life-threatening condition where the stomach fills with gas and twists. To prevent this, encourage your dog to take short breaks and drink in moderation.

Planning hydration strategies for outdoor adventures is equally important. If you're heading out on a hike or a long day trip, research your route to ensure there are water sources along the way or pack enough water to meet both your needs and your dog's. **Cooling accessories** like bandanas, vests, or mats designed for dogs can also help regulate their body temperature and reduce the risk of overheating, lessening the strain on their hydration levels.

It's also a good idea to hydrate your dog before exercise. **Offering water 30 to 60 minutes before heading out** can ensure they start their activity well-hydrated without having a full stomach, which might cause discomfort during movement. Post-exercise hydration is equally critical. After your dog has cooled down, offer them water to help replenish fluids lost during activity and aid recovery.

Finally, be mindful of the environment. Asphalt and pavement can become extremely hot in the sun, not only risking paw pad burns but also reflecting heat upwards, increasing your dog's body temperature. Whenever possible, opt for shaded paths, grassy areas, or cooler times of the day to exercise. If your dog seems reluctant to continue walking or playing, never force them, as it could indicate they're overheating or becoming dehydrated.

Hydration for Senior Dogs

As dogs age, their bodies undergo changes that can affect their hydration needs and drinking habits. Senior dogs may have a reduced sense of thirst, which can lead to insufficient water intake and increase their vulnerability to dehydration. Chronic conditions that are more common in older dogs, such as kidney disease, diabetes, or arthritis, can also elevate their need for hydration or make accessing water more challenging. Ensuring your senior dog remains well-hydrated is crucial for their comfort, health, and quality of life.

One effective way to promote hydration in older dogs is by making water easily accessible. Placing multiple water bowls around your home can significantly increase the likelihood of your dog drinking regularly. This approach is especially helpful if your senior dog has mobility issues or finds it difficult to navigate stairs or long distances to reach a single water source. Choose **wide, shallow bowls** that are easy for your dog to use, particularly if they have arthritis or stiffness in their neck or back. For dogs with impaired vision, keeping water bowls in consistent, familiar locations can help them find and use them more easily.

In addition to accessibility, the quality of the water you provide matters. Clean, fresh water is more appealing to dogs, so be sure to change it at least once or twice a day. Some dogs prefer running water, so a pet water fountain can be an excellent option for encouraging hydration, as the flowing water may be more enticing and keeps water fresher for longer periods.

If your senior dog is still not drinking enough, you can boost their water intake through diet. Offering moisture-rich foods, such as wet dog food or homemade meals with higher water content, can be a simple yet effective solution. Adding a small amount of warm, unsalted chicken or beef broth to their water can make it more enticing, but ensure it is free from harmful ingredients like onions, garlic, or excessive sodium. For a refreshing treat, consider offering small amounts of ice cubes or even frozen broth cubes, which can also help alleviate minor discomfort from teething or oral issues, which are common in older dogs.

It's also important to monitor your senior dog for signs of dehydration, as they may not show obvious symptoms until the issue becomes more severe. Common signs to watch for include dry gums, sunken eyes, lethargy, reduced skin elasticity (where the skin doesn't spring back quickly when gently pinched), and dark or concentrated urine. If you notice any of these symptoms, prompt action is necessary. Encourage your dog to drink water or seek veterinary advice if the dehydration seems significant or if your dog is experiencing underlying health issues.

Encouraging hydration in senior dogs also requires a holistic approach to their environment and daily routine. Ensure that their resting areas are comfortable and cool, particularly during warm weather, as older dogs may struggle to regulate their body temperature. Avoid overexertion during walks or playtime, and always have water on hand to offer during breaks.

In the next chapter we will discuss another fundamental component of dog nutrition: vitamins and minerals.

Chapter 3: Vitamins and minerals

Vitamins and minerals are indispensable for your dog's overall health, acting as the foundational support system for a wide array of bodily functions. From strengthening bones and supporting the nervous system to facilitating energy production and maintaining proper immune function, these nutrients are critical for keeping your dog active, healthy, and thriving. Unlike macronutrients like proteins, fats, and carbohydrates, which the body can sometimes synthesize or use as a flexible energy source, **most vitamins and minerals cannot be produced in sufficient quantities by your dog's body**. As a result, they must be consistently supplied through a balanced diet to prevent deficiencies that could lead to long-term health issues.

The Importance of Vitamins

Vitamins are organic compounds required in small but crucial amounts to sustain life and promote optimal body function. Dogs need both fat-soluble and water-soluble vitamins, each playing distinct roles in their overall health.

Fat-soluble vitamins, including Vitamins A, D, E, and K, are stored in the fatty tissues and liver. Vitamin A is essential for maintaining good vision, supporting immune defenses, and ensuring healthy skin and coat. It is found in ingredients such as carrots, sweet potatoes, and spinach, which provide beta-carotene, a precursor to Vitamin A. Vitamin D is critical for calcium and phosphorus regulation, which ensures the development of strong bones and teeth. Exposure to sunlight and consumption of fish or fortified foods can help meet this need. Vitamin E, a potent antioxidant, protects cells from oxidative damage, promoting healthy skin and a robust immune system. It is found in seeds, nuts, and vegetable oils. Vitamin K is necessary for blood clotting and can be naturally sourced from leafy greens like kale and spinach.

Water-soluble vitamins, including the B-complex group and Vitamin C, are not stored in the body, and must be consumed daily. The B-complex vitamins (B1, B2, B3, B5, B6, B7, B12, and folic acid) are vital for energy metabolism, red blood cell production, and proper functioning of the nervous system. These are found in a variety of sources, such as lean meats, fish, and whole grains. Vitamin C, meanwhile, acts as an antioxidant and plays a key role in collagen synthesis, aiding in wound healing and maintaining skin elasticity. Although dogs can synthesize small amounts of Vitamin C on their own, including it in their diet through fruits like blueberries or apples can provide additional benefits.

The Role of Minerals

Minerals, inorganic elements required for numerous biological processes, are divided into two categories: **macro-minerals and trace minerals**. While macro-minerals are needed in larger amounts, trace minerals are equally critical despite being required in smaller quantities.

Key macro-minerals include **calcium, phosphorus, magnesium, sodium, chloride, potassium, and sulfur**. Calcium and phosphorus work together to ensure strong bones and teeth, with the ideal balance being about 1.2 parts calcium to 1 part phosphorus. Magnesium supports muscle function and nerve signaling, while potassium and sodium maintain fluid balance and prevent dehydration. These minerals can be found in ingredients such as bone meal, eggshell powder, leafy greens, and bananas.

Trace minerals include **iron, zinc, copper, selenium, and iodine**. Iron is crucial for oxygen transport in the blood, supporting energy levels and overall vitality. Zinc is essential for immune health, wound healing, and maintaining a shiny coat. Copper plays a role in iron absorption and red blood cell formation. Selenium, a powerful antioxidant, protects cells from damage and supports thyroid function. Iodine, primarily sourced from seafood or iodized salt, is vital for regulating thyroid hormones, which control metabolism.

Balancing Vitamins and Minerals Homemade Foods

Achieving the right balance of vitamins and minerals in your dog's homemade diet requires careful consideration. While many natural ingredients are rich in these nutrients, their bioavailability—the ease with which the body can absorb and use them—can vary. For example, calcium from bone meal or eggshell powder is more readily absorbed than calcium from raw bones. Chelated minerals, which are bound to amino acids, also tend to have higher bioavailability compared to non-chelated forms.

Including a diverse range of vegetables and fruits in your dog's meals can help ensure they receive a wide spectrum of these nutrients. Leafy greens like spinach, kale, and Swiss chard are excellent sources of Vitamins A, C, and K, while carrots provide beta-carotene, which is converted into Vitamin A. Fruits like blueberries, apples, and cranberries are rich in antioxidants, supporting immune health and combating free radicals that can accelerate aging and cellular damage.

Safety Considerations and Next Steps

While providing a variety of nutrient-dense foods is essential, it's equally important to be mindful of ingredients that can be harmful to dogs. Some fruits and vegetables, such as grapes, raisins, onions, and garlic, are toxic and should be avoided. Additionally, excessive supplementation of fat-soluble vitamins, like Vitamin A or D, can lead to toxicity, as these are stored in the body rather than excreted.

In the next chapter, we will explore a comprehensive guide to toxic foods, ensuring you know exactly what to avoid when crafting meals for your furry friend. This knowledge will empower you to confidently provide meals that are not only delicious but also perfectly suited to your dog's nutritional needs.

Chapter 4: Toxic Foods for Your Dog

As loving pet owners, we often want to share the foods we enjoy with our furry companions. However, not all human foods are safe for dogs, and some can be downright dangerous. Understanding which foods are toxic to dogs is essential to ensure their safety and well-being. In this chapter, we'll explore common foods that should never find their way into your dog's diet and explain why they pose a risk.

Chocolate and Caffeine

Chocolate is one of the most well-known toxic foods for dogs, containing **theobromine and caffeine**—compounds that dogs cannot metabolize efficiently. Dark chocolate, baking chocolate, and cocoa powder are particularly dangerous due to their high concentrations of these substances. Symptoms of chocolate toxicity include vomiting, diarrhea, rapid breathing, increased heart rate, seizures, and in severe cases, death. Always keep chocolate and caffeinated products like coffee or tea out of your dog's reach.

Grapes and Raisins

Grapes and raisins, even in small quantities, **can cause acute kidney failure** in dogs. While the exact toxic component remains unknown, it's clear that these fruits pose a significant risk. Early symptoms include vomiting, diarrhea, lethargy, and a loss of appetite. If left untreated, kidney failure can set in, leading to serious health complications. Never offer grapes or raisins as a treat and be cautious with foods like trail mixes and baked goods that might contain them.

Onions, Garlic, and Allium Family Plants

Onions, garlic, leeks, and chives—**all members of the allium family**—are toxic to dogs. These foods contain compounds that can damage red blood cells, leading to anemia. Symptoms may not appear immediately but can include weakness, lethargy, pale gums, and an increased heart rate. Cooked, raw, or powdered forms of these plants are all dangerous, so avoid feeding them to your dog or using them in homemade dog food recipes.

Xylitol

Xylitol is a sugar substitute found in sugar-free gum, candies, baked goods, and some peanut butters. Ingesting even a small amount can cause a rapid release of insulin, leading to **life-threatening hypoglycemia (low blood sugar)**. Symptoms of xylitol poisoning include vomiting, loss of coordination, seizures, and liver failure. Always check ingredient labels and keep sugar-free products well out of your dog's reach.

Alcohol

Alcohol and products containing alcohol can be extremely toxic to dogs. Even small amounts can cause vomiting, diarrhea, coordination problems, difficulty breathing, and in severe cases, coma, or death. Be cautious with alcoholic beverages, as well as foods prepared with alcohol, such as rum-soaked cakes.

Avocado

Avocados contain **persin**, a compound toxic to many animals, including dogs. While dogs are generally less sensitive to persin than some other animals, ingestion can still cause vomiting and diarrhea. Additionally, the large pit poses a choking hazard or can cause intestinal blockages if swallowed. It's best to avoid feeding avocado to your dog altogether.

Macadamia Nuts

Macadamia nuts are highly toxic to dogs, even in small quantities. Ingestion can cause symptoms such as weakness, vomiting, tremors, and hyperthermia. These symptoms typically appear within 12 hours of ingestion and can last up to 48 hours. Keep macadamia nuts and foods containing them away from your dog.

Raw Yeast Dough

Raw yeast dough can expand in a dog's stomach, causing **painful bloating** and potentially life-threatening complications. Additionally, as the yeast ferments, it produces alcohol, which can lead to alcohol poisoning. Never allow your dog to consume raw dough and dispose of any scraps carefully.

Certain Fruits with Seeds or Pits

Fruits like cherries, peaches, plums, and apples contain seeds or pits that can be harmful to dogs. The seeds and pits often contain cyanogenic compounds that release cyanide when metabolized. Swallowing pits can also cause choking or intestinal blockages. If offering fruit as a treat, always remove any seeds or pits beforehand.

Avoiding toxic foods is just one part of keeping your dog healthy. Ensuring that the meals you prepare meet their nutritional needs is equally important. Even the best-intentioned homemade meals can lack the balance necessary for your dog's long-term health. That's where the **Association of American Feed Control Officials (AAFCO) standards** come in.

In the next chapter, we'll explore these guidelines, which are designed to help you create meals that are not only safe but also nutritionally complete.

Chapter 5: The AAFCO Standards

Dogs' nutritional needs evolve as they age and if they have specific health conditions. Puppies, pregnant or nursing dogs, and active breeds require more calories and nutrients than adult dogs in maintenance mode. Similarly, dogs facing health challenges such as kidney disease or obesity may require diets tailored to their needs. Understanding AAFCO standards aids in adjusting homemade recipes to accommodate these varying requirements.

The Association of American Feed Control Officials (AAFCO) establishes guidelines and standards to **ensure the nutritional adequacy of pet foods**, including those made at home. Understanding these standards is essential for anyone interested in crafting balanced and nutritious meals for their dogs. In fact, it is fundamentally important that your dog's diet meet these standards, whether it is through homemade or commercial food. AAFCO provides nutrient profiles for various life stages of dogs, such as growth, reproduction, and adult maintenance, as well as for all life stages. These profiles specify the minimum needs for essential nutrients like proteins, fats, vitamins, and minerals, which are vital to meet the unique requirements of dogs throughout their lives.

Minimum Protein Content

AAFCO standards outline the minimum protein content needed for dogs, which varies depending on their life stage.

- 🐾 Food for **puppies** should contain at least 22.5% protein to support their rapid growth and development
- 🐾 Food for **growth** and reproduction should have a minimum of 22.5%
- 🐾 Food for **adult maintenance** must contain at least 18% protein on a dry matter basis

🐾 For **senior dogs**, while there is no specific percentage mandated, it is generally recommended to maintain a protein level like that of adult maintenance to help preserve muscle mass and overall health.

Minimum Fat Content

Fats play a key role in a dog's diet, providing energy and supporting cellular function. AAFCO recommends a **minimum of 5.5% fat for adult maintenance and 8.5% for growth and reproduction.**

Minimum Carbohydrates Content

For puppies and pregnant or nursing dogs, carbohydrates can help support their high energy needs and overall development. For adult dogs, carbohydrates can contribute to a balanced diet, helping to maintain energy levels and support overall health. While AAFCO does not specify a minimum carbohydrate requirement, it is generally recommended that carbohydrates make up a significant portion of a dog's diet, particularly for those in growth and reproduction stages. This typically means that carbohydrates **should constitute around 30% to 50% of the total caloric intake** in a balanced diet. This range helps ensure that dogs receive adequate energy to support their high activity levels and developmental needs during these critical life stages. Furthermore, including sources such as whole grains, vegetables, and fruits can provide not only energy but also fiber, which is important for healthy digestion.

Minimum Vitamins and Minerals Content

The AAFCO standards outline specific requirements for essential vitamins and minerals that are crucial for a dog's health at various life stages. In fact, vitamins and minerals play vital roles in bone health, immune function, and overall well-being.

For **adult dogs**, the minimum requirements include:
🐾 Calcium: 0.5% on a dry matter basis
🐾 Phosphorus: 0.4% on a dry matter basis
🐾 Vitamin A: 5,000 IU/kg
🐾 Vitamin D: 500 IU/kg
🐾 Vitamin E: 50 IU/kg

- Vitamin K: 0.2 mg/kg
- Thiamine (Vitamin B1): 1.0 mg/kg
- Riboflavin (Vitamin B2): 2.0 mg/kg
- Niacin (Vitamin B3): 10.0 mg/kg
- Pyridoxine (Vitamin B6): 1.0 mg/kg
- Cobalamin (Vitamin B12): 0.02 mg/kg
- Folic Acid: 0.1 mg/kg
- Pantothenic Acid: 5.0 mg/kg
- Iron: 80 mg/kg
- Zinc: 120 mg/kg
- Copper: 7.3 mg/kg
- Manganese: 0.5 mg/kg
- Selenium: 0.11 mg/kg
- Iodine: 0.3 mg/kg

For **puppies, pregnant, or nursing dogs**, the requirements are higher to support growth and development:
- Calcium: 1.0% on a dry matter basis
- Phosphorus: 0.8% on a dry matter basis
- Vitamin A: 10,000 IU/kg
- Vitamin D: 1,000 IU/kg
- Vitamin E: 100 IU/kg
- Vitamin K: 0.3 mg/kg
- Thiamine (Vitamin B1): 1.5 mg/kg
- Riboflavin (Vitamin B2): 2.5 mg/kg
- Niacin (Vitamin B3): 10.0 mg/kg
- Pyridoxine (Vitamin B6): 1.0 mg/kg
- Cobalamin (Vitamin B12): 0.02 mg/kg
- Folic Acid: 0.1 mg/kg
- Pantothenic Acid: 5.0 mg/kg
- Iron: 80 mg/kg
- Zinc: 120 mg/kg
- Copper: 7.3 mg/kg
- Manganese: 0.5 mg/kg
- Selenium: 0.11 mg/kg
- Iodine: 0.3 mg/kg

Your Dog's Life Stage

As you now know, understanding the different life stages of your dog is crucial for providing the right nutrition tailored to their specific needs. But how do you determine your dog's life stage?

The journey begins with **puppyhood**, which spans **from birth to 12 months**. During this vibrant phase, puppies experience rapid growth and development, requiring a diet rich in protein and fat to fuel their energetic play and support the formation of strong muscles, bones, and teeth.

As your dog transitions into **adulthood**, typically recognized **from ages 1 to 7 years**, their nutritional focus shifts. Adult dogs need a balanced diet that maintains a healthy weight and supports overall well-being, reflecting their decreased energy requirements compared to their puppy days.

Finally, as dogs enter their **senior years**, generally **starting at 7 years of age**, their dietary needs evolve once more. Senior dogs often require lower-calorie diets that still provide high-quality protein to help preserve muscle mass while addressing specific health concerns such as joint health and digestion.

NOTE: When incorporating any commercial ingredients into your homemade dog food, knowing how to read pet food labels is important. AAFCO standards require labels to provide a guaranteed analysis of the minimum percentages of crude protein and fat, as well as the maximum percentages of crude fiber and moisture. This information guides you in determining if a commercial product meets your dog's dietary requirements and how it fits into the overall nutritional profile of your homemade recipes. In the next chapter we will talk more about food labels and how to read them properly.

Chapter 6: Reading Pet Food Labels for Nutrition

Navigating the world of pet food labels can initially feel overwhelming, but gaining some knowledge about what to look for allows you to make informed choices regarding the commercial ingredients you might want to add to your homemade dog food. Understanding pet food labels for nutritional quality requires familiarity with the terminology and the guidelines set by the AAFCO. This insight ensures that the commercial products you choose to enhance your homemade recipes align with the high standards you envision for your dog's diet.

Pay attention to the **product name**, which provides immediate insight into the primary ingredients. According to AAFCO regulations, if a product is named "*Chicken Dog Food*," chicken must account for **at least 95% of the total weight**, excluding water content. If the name includes a mix of ingredients, like "*Chicken and Rice Dog Food*," those two ingredients together must make up 95% of the total weight, with the primary ingredient listed first. This guideline helps ensure that the product mainly consists of the specified ingredients, giving you a clear picture of its composition.

The guaranteed analysis on the label plays a vital role in assessing the nutritional content of the pet food. This section outlines the minimum percentages of crude protein and crude fat, along with the maximum percentages of crude fiber and moisture. These figures provide a snapshot of the food's nutritional profile, allowing you to compare it against AAFCO's minimum requirements for your dog's life stage. For example, if you're preparing food for a growing puppy, confirm that any commercial products you use meet or exceed AAFCO's recommended protein and fat levels for growth and reproduction.

To illustrate, consider a hypothetical dog food label for "*Premium Chicken and Brown Rice Recipe.*" The guaranteed analysis might read:
- 🐾 Crude Protein: 30% (minimum)
- 🐾 Crude Fat: 18% (minimum)
- 🐾 Crude Fiber: 5% (maximum)
- 🐾 Moisture: 10% (maximum)

In this example, the protein content is quite high, which is beneficial for a growing puppy that requires more protein for muscle development. The fat content is also substantial, providing the necessary energy for active growth. The fiber content is within a reasonable range, supporting healthy digestion, while the moisture level indicates that the food is not overly dry, which can be important for hydration.

The ingredient list on pet food labels serves as a valuable tool for evaluating quality. **Ingredients are listed in descending order by weight**, meaning the first few ingredients are the most significant in the food. High-quality dog foods typically feature a protein source, such as chicken, beef, or lamb, as the first ingredient. For our example, if the first ingredient is "*Chicken,*" followed by "*Brown Rice,*" and then "*Carrots,*" this indicates a good balance of protein and carbohydrates, with added nutrients from vegetables. **Look for whole food ingredients** and avoid products with excessive fillers, artificial colors, or preservatives, which can diminish the food's nutritional value. The closer the ingredients are to their natural state, the more nutritious they will be for your dog.

The AAFCO statement of nutritional adequacy or purpose represents a key element of the label. This statement indicates whether the food is formulated to meet the nutritional levels established by the AAFCO Dog Food Nutrient Profiles for a specific life stage, such as growth, reproduction, adult maintenance, or all life stages. For instance, if the label states, "*Formulated to meet the nutritional levels established by AAFCO for all life stages,*" it confirms that the food provides a complete and balanced diet for your dog, according to recognized standards. Selecting commercial products that align with your dog's life stage ensures they receive the necessary nutrients in the right proportions.

Understanding the **caloric content per serving**, typically listed as kilocalories per kilogram (kcal/kg) or kilocalories per cup, helps maintain your dog's ideal weight. This information aids you in accurately calculating how much commercial food to include in your dog's diet, ensuring they receive the energy they need without overfeeding.

For example, if the "*Premium Chicken and Brown Rice Recipe*" label indicates that it contains 400 kcal per cup, and you plan to feed your dog a total of 2 cups of food per day, you would be providing 800 kcal from this commercial food alone. If your dog requires 1,200 kcal daily based on their weight and activity level, you will need to supplement with additional homemade food or treats that provide the remaining 400 kcal, ensuring a balanced and nutritious diet.

Chapter 7: Transitioning to Homemade Dog Food

Switching your dog to a homemade diet is a rewarding journey, but it's important to approach the **transition carefully** to ensure success. A sudden change in diet can cause digestive upset, stress, or rejection of the new food, especially if your dog has been eating commercial kibble for most of their life. By taking a gradual, methodical approach, you can help your dog adjust to their new meals comfortably and safely.

Why Transitioning Gradually Matters

Dogs thrive on consistency, and their digestive systems are highly sensitive to sudden changes in diet. Abruptly introducing homemade food can lead to symptoms such as diarrhea, vomiting, or loss of appetite. Transitioning slowly allows your dog's **digestive system to adapt to new ingredients, flavors, and textures**, minimizing the risk of gastrointestinal upset. It also gives you an opportunity to monitor how your dog responds to the new diet and adjust as needed.

The Step-by-Step Transition Plan

The following steps provide a practical guide to transitioning your dog to homemade food.

1. Start with a Small Portion of Homemade Food

Begin by mixing a small amount of homemade food into your dog's current diet. **A good starting ratio is 25% homemade food and 75% of their regular food**. Mix the two together thoroughly to encourage your dog to eat both.

2. Gradually Increase the Homemade Food

Over the next 7-10 days, slowly increase the proportion of homemade food while decreasing the amount of commercial food.
For example:
- 🐾 Days 1-3: 25% homemade food, 75% commercial food
- 🐾 Days 4-6: 50% homemade food, 50% commercial food
- 🐾 Days 7-9: 75% homemade food, 25% commercial food
- 🐾 Day 10: 100% homemade food

Monitor your dog closely during this process. If you notice signs of digestive upset, such as loose stools or a reduced appetite, slow down the transition and allow their system more time to adjust.

3. Offer Consistent Mealtimes

Feed your dog at the same times each day to create a sense of routine. Dogs are creatures of habit, and maintaining consistent meal times helps them adapt to the new diet more easily.

Signs of a Successful Transition

A successful transition becomes evident through several clear signs. Your dog's stool should be firm and well-formed, a strong indicator that their digestive system is adapting well to the new diet. They should exhibit **steady energy levels**, maintaining their usual activity and enthusiasm for daily routines. Over time, you may notice improvements in their coat and skin, with **a glossier coat and healthier skin** reflecting the benefits of a balanced homemade diet. Furthermore, an eager appetite signals that your dog is enjoying and accepting their new meals without hesitation.

However, if your dog displays prolonged digestive issues, decreased energy, or visible discomfort, it's important to consult your veterinarian. Such symptoms could suggest an intolerance or sensitivity to certain ingredients that may need to be adjusted.

Introducing New Ingredients

When creating a homemade diet, it's important to **introduce new ingredients one at a time**. This allows you to monitor how your dog reacts to each component and identify any potential allergies or intolerances.
For example, if you're adding sweet potatoes to their meals for the first time, include a small amount initially and observe their reaction over several days before adding another new ingredient.

Special Considerations for Puppies and Senior Dogs

The transition process may require additional care for puppies and senior dogs, as their nutritional needs and digestive systems differ from those of adult dogs.

Puppies

Because puppies grow rapidly, their bodies **demand a diet rich in protein, fats, and calories to support their intense growth** and high energy levels. Proper nutrition during this critical stage helps develop strong muscles, bones, and a robust immune system. Transitioning puppies to a homemade diet should be done gradually, as their digestive systems are still developing and sensitive to sudden changes. **Begin with small portions of homemade food and increase the quantity slowly over two weeks or more.** Monitor their weight gain and energy levels regularly, ensuring they are meeting developmental milestones. Look for signs of healthy growth, such as bright eyes, a shiny coat, and active behavior. Frequent veterinary check-ups are essential during this period to verify that their nutritional needs are being met and to adjust the diet if necessary.

Senior Dogs

Older dogs often face unique challenges, such as reduced appetites, slower metabolism, and specific health concerns like arthritis or kidney disease. These factors make a tailored approach to their homemade diet crucial. Senior dogs benefit from **meals that are lower in calories** to prevent weight gain but still provide high-quality protein to preserve muscle mass. Additional considerations include including ingredients that support joint health, such as **omega-3 fatty acids and glucosamine**, and ensuring the diet is easy to chew and digest. Regular vet consultations are vital to adapt the diet to any emerging health conditions and to monitor their overall well-being. Making **water-rich meals** and offering smaller, more frequent portions can also help maintain hydration and accommodate their changing appetites.

Tips for Picky Eaters

Some dogs may be hesitant to try new foods, especially if they're accustomed to the taste and texture of kibble. To encourage your dog to eat homemade food, consider several strategies to make the experience more enjoyable and appealing for them.

Warming the food slightly can significantly enhance its aroma, making it more enticing for your dog. This simple step stimulates their sense of smell, which plays a key role in their appetite and can be particularly helpful for dogs that rely on scent cues when deciding what to eat. Adding a small amount of low-sodium broth to the food introduces a familiar and appealing flavor that many dogs find irresistible, especially if they have a history of enjoying savory treats.

For dogs hesitant to fully embrace the change, **mixing in a favorite treat or a small portion of their usual food** can create a sense of familiarity, helping to ease the transition. This gradual blending of flavors and textures allows your dog to explore the new food without feeling overwhelmed. Additionally, incorporating small, dog-safe garnishes such as shredded chicken or a sprinkle of Parmesan cheese can encourage a more positive response to their meals.

Presentation can also make a difference. Serving the food in their usual bowl or a new dish designated for special meals can create a sense of excitement or comfort. Offering food at consistent mealtimes reinforces a routine, which many dogs thrive on. Be patient and persistent during this process, consistently offering the food without forcing it. Some dogs may take several tries before accepting the new diet, so maintaining a calm and encouraging attitude is key. Allow your dog to explore the new flavors and textures at their own pace and celebrate small successes along the way.

For particularly stubborn eaters, introducing **homemade meals as treats or snacks before transitioning** them fully to the new diet can help build familiarity and trust. Experimenting with different textures, such as pureeing vegetables or shredding meats, may also help cater to your dog's individual preferences. This gentle persistence helps strengthen their curiosity and encourages a lasting acceptance of their new diet.

To make the transition process more convenient, consider **batch-cooking meals** and storing them in portioned containers. This ensures consistency in your dog's diet and saves time in the kitchen. We will discuss this further in the next chapter.

Chapter 8: Batch Cooking and Meal Prep Tips

Preparing homemade dog food doesn't have to be a daily challenge. By adopting batch cooking and smart meal prep strategies, you can save time and ensure your dog always has access to fresh, nutritious meals. Batch cooking allows you to prepare several days or even weeks of meals at once, making homemade dog food convenient and sustainable, even for busy schedules.

Batch cooking simplifies the process of feeding your dog a homemade diet by **minimizing the time spent cooking each day**. Preparing meals in larger quantities ensures consistency in your dog's diet and reduces the likelihood of running out of food unexpectedly. Additionally, batch cooking provides an opportunity to **carefully measure ingredients**, ensuring each meal is nutritionally balanced and portioned appropriately for your dog's size, age, and activity level. It's also a cost-effective approach, as buying ingredients in bulk often reduces expenses.

Getting Started with Batch Cooking

To begin batch cooking, **start by planning your dog's meals for the week or month**. Use the recipes provided in this book to create a structured meal plan, **rotating the recipes suitable for your dog type weight**. Decide which recipes you'll prepare and create a detailed shopping list of ingredients, prioritizing fresh, high-quality produce, lean meats, and nutrient-rich add-ins like spinach or pumpkin. Once you have your ingredients, allocate a dedicated time for meal prep, such as a weekend morning, to streamline the process and ensure consistency.

Investing in the right tools can make batch cooking more efficient and enjoyable. Essential items include a **large cutting board** for chopping vegetables, **sharp knives** for precise cuts, and a **food scale** to measure ingredients accurately. Measuring cups, mixing bowls, and a slow cooker or Instant Pot can simplify cooking, especially for stews or recipes requiring tender meat and soft vegetables. Freezer-safe containers or resealable bags allow you to portion and store meals efficiently, while labels help you keep track of preparation dates and recipe types.

Efficient Meal Prep Techniques

Start by washing and prepping all ingredients. For example, peel and dice sweet potatoes, chop leafy greens, and trim excess fat from chicken or beef. Cooking ingredients in bulk is a game-changer—you can steam a large pot of vegetables while boiling grains like brown rice or quinoa in another. At the same time, you can bake or slow-cook proteins like chicken thighs or fish fillets, ensuring all components are ready simultaneously.

Once the ingredients are prepared, **combine them according to the recipes in this book**, ensuring each batch contains the proper proportions of proteins, fats, carbohydrates, and essential vitamins and minerals. For example, when preparing the Turkey and Veggie Delight, layer cooked turkey, steamed veggies, and rice in each portion, adding the sunflower oil.

Portioning the food is a crucial step to ensure your dog receives the appropriate amount of nutrients and calories. Use a food scale to measure servings based on your dog's weight and energy needs, following the instructions provided in the next chapter. Pre-portioning meals ensures convenience and consistency, especially on busy days.

Proper storage is essential to maintain the freshness and safety of homemade dog food. Divide cooked meals into individual portions and store them in airtight containers or resealable freezer bags. **Label each container with the preparation date, recipe name, and portion size** to simplify feeding time. Meals can be stored in the refrigerator for up to three days or frozen for up to three months.

To save freezer space, consider flattening freezer bags for easy stacking. If you prefer containers, **opt for stackable, BPA-free options to maximize space,** and keep your storage area organized. Designate a specific shelf in your refrigerator or freezer for dog food to avoid confusion and ensure easy access.

When it's time to serve frozen meals, **transfer the portion to the refrigerator the night before** to allow it to thaw gradually. For quicker thawing, place the sealed bag in cold water for about 30 minutes. Avoid microwaving homemade dog food, as uneven heating can create hot spots that may burn your dog's mouth. Instead, warm the food gently on the stovetop or serve it at room temperature.

Before serving, give the food a good stir to distribute moisture and flavors evenly. Check the temperature to ensure it's safe and palatable for your dog. Consistent presentation helps your dog look forward to meals, reinforcing positive mealtime habits.

Rotating Recipes and Ingredients

Variety is key to keeping your dog's meals exciting and nutritionally complete. Rotating recipes from this book, ensures your dog receives a broad range of nutrients. Batch cooking different recipes in advance allows you to alternate meals throughout the week, preventing boredom and providing balanced nutrition with minimal effort.

Safety and Hygiene

Maintaining hygiene during meal prep is crucial for food safety. Wash your hands thoroughly before and after handling raw ingredients, especially meats. Use separate cutting boards for raw and cooked items to prevent cross-contamination. Regularly clean utensils and kitchen surfaces with hot, soapy water.

Ensure that prepared meals are stored at the correct temperatures. Refrigerated food should be kept at or below 40°F (4°C), and frozen food should remain at 0°F (-18°C) or colder. Periodically inspect storage containers for cracks or damage that could harbor bacteria. Discard any meals showing signs of spoilage, such as an off smell, discoloration, or mold.

Batch Cooking Tips for Beginners

Starting your batch cooking journey can feel overwhelming at first, but with a few simple strategies, you'll quickly develop a routine that works for both you and your dog. The key is to begin with manageable steps and build confidence over time.

If you're new to batch cooking, it's best to start with one or two simple recipes from this book. Choose meals that require minimal preparation and ingredients to help you ease into the process. **Aim for a week's worth of food initially rather than committing to a full month right away**. As you gain confidence and efficiency, you can gradually increase the batch size.

A helpful way to refine your batch cooking skills is by keeping a journal. **Record your dog's reactions to different meals**, noting their favorite flavors, portion sizes, and any positive changes in their health. If your dog experiences increased energy, a shinier coat, or improved digestion, these are signs that you're on the right track. By documenting your process, you'll quickly learn which ingredients and cooking methods work best for your dog.

Once you've prepared a couple of successful batches, **consider establishing a routine that fits your schedule**. Some pet owners prefer cooking all meals at once over the weekend, while others break up the process into two or three smaller sessions throughout the week. Find a rhythm that aligns with your availability and stick to it.

To make batch cooking even more efficient, **group tasks together.** For instance, wash and chop all vegetables before moving on to cooking proteins. If possible, use multiple cooking methods at the same time—steam vegetables while baking meats or cooking grains in a separate pot. Organizing your workflow in a logical sequence reduces prep time and helps ensure all ingredients are ready when you need them.

As you become more comfortable with batch cooking, you can start tailoring meals to your dog's specific needs. Consider factors such as age, breed, activity level, and dietary preferences. Some dogs require higher protein content, while others may benefit from more fiber-rich vegetables. Experimenting with ingredient ratios will help you create well-balanced meals suited to your dog's lifestyle.

Chapter 9: Recipes

In this chapter, we present a selection of homemade recipes designed to meet the diverse dietary needs of dogs. These recipes include options for active and non-active animals, hypoallergenic diets, vegetarian choices, and raw food preparations, providing a convenient and nutritious alternative to commercial pet diets. While these recipes serve as a useful resource, they should not replace a dedicated nutritional plan tailored to your dog's specific health requirements. Instead, they offer a temporary solution while applying the knowledge acquired from previous chapters to ensure balanced meals.

The suggested diet is formulated to be provided daily and should be divided into multiple meals to maintain consistent energy levels throughout the day. All ingredient measurements should be based on their raw weight to maintain accurate nutritional values. Additionally, dietary supplements can be incorporated to ensure each meal meets the dog's complete nutritional needs.

Tips to Prepare Homemade Meals

The Best Protein Sources

Meat and fish serve as the primary protein sources and should be cooked using safe methods such as steaming, grilling, or simmering with a small amount of water. Raw meat can also be included, but only if it is high-quality beef that has been frozen for at least 48 hours to eliminate potential pathogens. Organ meats, including heart, kidneys, lungs, and spleen, can provide additional nutrients; however, liver should be used sparingly to avoid excessive vitamin A intake.

Carbohydrates for Energy and Fiber

Carbohydrates are essential in a balanced diet and can be sourced from various grains and gluten-free alternatives. Traditional options include pasta, small pasta shapes, couscous, and whole grains for additional fiber content. Gluten-free choices such as potatoes, polenta, rice, quinoa, and tapioca are excellent substitutes for dogs with sensitivities. When preparing grains, they should be cooked thoroughly but not excessively; cooking them slightly longer than the packaging instructions suggests can aid digestibility. Unlike human meal preparation, rinsing grains after cooking is not necessary unless during the initial dietary transition phases.

Vegetables for Digestive Health and Nutrients

Vegetables play an important role in your dog's diet by providing fiber, vitamins, and minerals. Suitable vegetables include carrots, zucchini, green beans, chard, chicory, spinach, and lettuce. The number of vegetables in meals can be adjusted based on stool consistency to maintain healthy digestion. Vegetables should be properly cooked, peeled if necessary, and blended to ensure easy digestion, particularly for dogs with sensitive stomachs.

Fruits as Occasional Treats

Fruits can be included as a nutritious and enjoyable reward. However, fruits with high fructose content, such as bananas, melons, and watermelon, should be given in moderation as they can impact stool consistency. Always introduce fruits gradually and observe any digestive changes to determine suitable portion sizes for your dog.

Healthy Fats for Essential Nutrients

Fats contribute to energy levels and coat health and should be selected carefully. Recommended sources include sunflower oil, corn oil, olive oil, and salmon oil. Butter and lard may also be used in small quantities as alternatives. It is essential to maintain a balanced intake of fats without replacing or eliminating key ingredients in recipes. Properly mixing ingredients ensures that dogs consume all components rather than selectively eating their preferred elements.

By following these guidelines and using the homemade recipes in this book, you can provide your dog with wholesome, balanced meals tailored to their specific dietary requirements. Paying close attention to portion sizes, cooking methods, and ingredient choices will help maintain your dog's overall health and well-being.

Recipes for Active Adult Dogs

A ctive dogs require **nutrient-dense meals** that provide **sustained energy**, promote **muscle recovery**, and support **overall health**. Whether your dog enjoys long walks, hiking, agility training, or simply has a naturally high energy level, a well-balanced diet is essential to fuel their daily activities.

These recipes are specifically designed for **active adult dogs**, incorporating **lean proteins, complex carbohydrates, and healthy fats** to support **muscle development, endurance, and optimal performance**. Each meal contains **high-quality, natural ingredients** that provide essential nutrients without unnecessary fillers or artificial additives.

Every dog's **energy expenditure varies based on their breed, weight, and daily activity level**. These recipes include **conversion tables**, making it easy to adjust portion sizes to match your dog's **specific caloric needs**. Whether your dog is moderately active or highly energetic, these meals can be tailored to provide the right balance of **protein, fats, and carbohydrates**.

Dogs that engage in **regular exercise, running, or agility training** require meals that support **muscle endurance and post-activity recovery**. Including **lean meats, healthy fats, and complex carbohydrates** in their diet helps maintain **muscle mass**, replenishes **energy stores**, and prevents **fatigue**.

Turkey & Veggie Delight

A wholesome and nourishing meal packed with lean turkey, hearty rice, and a medley of fresh vegetables.

> This recipe is suitable for an **11-pound dog** with a daily caloric requirement of **370 calories**. Use the conversion tables to adjust the quantity based on your dog's weight.

Ingredients:
- 🐾 Turkey breast – 3.5 oz (cooked and shredded)
- 🐾 Rice – 1.8 oz (cooked)
- 🐾 Sunflower oil – 2 teaspoons
- 🐾 Vegetables (carrot, zucchini, and green beans) – 2.1 oz (finely chopped and lightly steamed)
- 🐾 Bread – 0.7 oz (crumbled)

Instructions:
1. Cook the turkey breast in a pan with a little water until fully cooked. Shred it into small, manageable pieces.
2. In a separate pot, cook the rice according to package instructions.
3. Lightly steam the carrot, zucchini, and green beans until soft but not mushy.
4. In a bowl, combine the cooked turkey, rice, and vegetables.
5. Add sunflower oil and mix well.
6. Crumble the bread and mix it in for texture.
7. Let it cool before serving.

Conversion table

Dog's Weight	Calories	Turkey breast	Rice	Sunflower oil (tsp)	Vegetables	Bread
22 lbs	600	7 oz	2.1 oz	4	2.1 oz	1.4 oz
33 lbs	840	7 oz	2.1 oz	6	2.1 oz	3.5 oz
44 lbs	1000	10.5 oz	2.8 oz	6	2.1 oz	3.5 oz
66 lbs	1400	17.5 oz	4.5 oz	8	3.5 oz	3.5 oz

Chicken & Pumpkin Power Bowl

A deliciously soft and easily digestible meal, perfect for dogs with sensitive stomachs.

> This recipe is suitable for an **11-pound dog** with a daily caloric requirement of **370 calories**. Use the conversion tables to adjust the quantity based on your dog's weight.

Ingredients:
- 🐾 Chicken breast – 3.5 oz (boiled and shredded)
- 🐾 Pasta – 1.8 oz (cooked)
- 🐾 Corn oil – 2 teaspoons
- 🐾 Vegetables (pumpkin and spinach) – 2.1 oz (mashed and finely chopped)
- 🐾 Bread – 0.7 oz (cubed and softened in warm water)

Instructions:
1. Boil the chicken breast until fully cooked, then shred it into small pieces.
2. Cook the pasta until soft.
3. Steam the pumpkin until it becomes mashable, and finely chop the spinach.
4. In a large bowl, mix the chicken, pasta, mashed pumpkin, and spinach.
5. Add corn oil and stir everything together.
6. Soak the bread in warm water, then mix it into the meal for a soft texture.
7. Let the dish cool before serving to your pup.

Conversion table

Dog's Weight	Calories	Chicken breast	Pasta	Corn oil (tsp)	Vegetables	Bread
22 lbs	600	7 oz	2.1 oz	4	2.1 oz	1.4 oz
33 lbs	840	7 oz	2.1 oz	6	2.1 oz	3.5 oz
44 lbs	1000	10.5 oz	2.8 oz	6	2.1 oz	3.5 oz
66 lbs	1400	17.5 oz	4.5 oz	8	3.5 oz	3.5 oz

Cod & Veggie Feast

A light yet nutrient-packed meal featuring delicate cod, wholesome rice, and a mix of fresh vegetables.

> This recipe is suitable for an **11-pound dog** with a daily caloric requirement of **370 calories**. Use the conversion tables to adjust the quantity based on your dog's weight.

Ingredients:
- 🐾 Cod – 4.9 oz (cooked and flaked)
- 🐾 Rice – 1.8 oz (cooked)
- 🐾 Sunflower oil – 2 teaspoons
- 🐾 Vegetables (carrot, zucchini, and green beans) – 2.1 oz (finely chopped and lightly steamed)
- 🐾 Bread – 0.7 oz (crumbled)

Instructions:
1. Boil or steam the cod until fully cooked, then flake it into small pieces.
2. Cook the rice separately.
3. Steam the carrot, zucchini, and green beans until soft.
4. In a bowl, combine the cooked cod, rice, and vegetables.
5. Drizzle sunflower oil over the mixture and stir well.
6. Crumble the bread and mix it in for extra texture.
7. Allow to cool before serving.

Conversion table

Dog's Weight	Calories	Cod	Rice	Sunflower oil (tsp)	Vegetables	Bread
22 lbs	600	7.7 oz	2.8 oz	4	2.1 oz	1.4 oz
33 lbs	840	8.5 oz	2.5 oz	6	2.1 oz	3.5 oz
44 lbs	1000	12.3 oz	3.2 oz	6	2.1 oz	3.5 oz
66 lbs	1400	21.1 oz	5.5 oz	8	3.5 oz	3.5 oz

Hake & Pumpkin Power Bowl

A soft, easily digestible meal that's great for sensitive stomachs.

This recipe is suitable for an **11-pound dog** with a daily caloric requirement of **370 calories**. Use the conversion tables to adjust the quantity based on your dog's weight.

Ingredients:
- Hake – 4.9 oz (boiled and flaked)
- Pasta – 1.8 oz (cooked)
- Sunflower oil – 2 teaspoons
- Vegetables (pumpkin and spinach) – 2.1 oz (mashed and finely chopped)
- Bread – 0.7 oz (cubed and softened in warm water)

Instructions:
1. Boil the hake until fully cooked, then flake it into small pieces.
2. Cook the pasta until soft.
3. Steam and mash the pumpkin, and finely chop the spinach.
4. In a large bowl, mix the hake, pasta, mashed pumpkin, and spinach.
5. Add sunflower oil and stir well.
6. Soak the bread in warm water, then mix it in for a soft texture.
7. Let the dish cool before serving.

Conversion table

Dog's Weight	Calories	Hake	Pasta	Sunflower oil (tsp)	Vegetables	Bread
22 lbs	600	7.7 oz	2.8 oz	4	2.1 oz	1.4 oz
33 lbs	840	8.5 oz	2.5 oz	6	2.1 oz	3.5 oz
44 lbs	1000	12.4 oz	3.2 oz	6	2.1 oz	3.5 oz
66 lbs	1400	21.2 oz	5.5 oz	8	3.5 oz	3.5 oz

Beef & Veggie Medley

A hearty and nutritious meal packed with lean beef, fiber-rich vegetables, and wholesome rice.

This recipe is suitable for an **11-pound dog** with a daily caloric requirement of **370 calories**. Use the conversion tables to adjust the quantity based on your dog's weight.

Ingredients:
- Lean beef fillet – 3.5 oz (cooked and finely chopped)
- Rice – 1.1 oz (cooked)
- Sunflower oil – 2 teaspoons
- Vegetables (carrot, zucchini, and green beans) – 2.1 oz (finely chopped and lightly steamed)
- Bread – 0.7 oz (crumbled)

Instructions:
1. Cook the lean beef fillet in a pan with a little water until fully cooked, then chop it into small pieces.
2. Cook the rice separately according to instructions.
3. Lightly steam the carrot, zucchini, and green beans until soft.
4. In a bowl, combine the cooked beef, rice, and vegetables.
5. Drizzle sunflower oil over the mixture and mix well.
6. Crumble the bread and mix it in for added texture.
7. Let it cool before serving.

Conversion table

Dog's Weight	Calories	Lean beef	Rice	Sunflower oil (tsp)	Vegetables	Bread
22 lbs	600	6.3 oz	1.4 oz	4	2.1 oz	1.4 oz
33 lbs	840	6.3 oz	1.7 oz	6	2.1 oz	3.5 oz
44 lbs	1000	8.8 oz	2.1 oz	6	2.1 oz	3.5 oz
66 lbs	1400	15.8 oz	2.8 oz	8	3.5 oz	3.5 oz

Pork & Pumpkin Delight

A delicious, soft, and digestible meal, perfect for dogs that love a little sweetness from pumpkin.

> This recipe is suitable for an **11-pound dog** with a daily caloric requirement of **370 calories**. Use the conversion tables to adjust the quantity based on your dog's weight.

Ingredients:
- 🐾 Lean pork fillet – 3.5 oz (boiled and shredded)
- 🐾 Pasta – 1.1 oz (cooked)
- 🐾 Corn oil – 2 teaspoons
- 🐾 Vegetables (pumpkin and spinach) – 2.1 oz (mashed and finely chopped)
- 🐾 Bread – 0.7 oz (cubed and softened in warm water)

Instructions:
1. Boil the pork fillet until fully cooked, then shred it into small, manageable pieces.
2. Cook the pasta until soft.
3. Steam and mash the pumpkin, and finely chop the spinach.
4. In a large bowl, mix the pork, pasta, mashed pumpkin, and spinach.
5. Add corn oil and stir well to combine.
6. Soak the bread in warm water, then mix it in for a softer texture.
7. Let the meal cool before serving to your pup.

Conversion table

Dog's Weight	Calories	Lean pork	Pasta	Corn oil (tsp)	Vegetables	Bread
22 lbs	600	6.3 oz	1.4 oz	4	2.1 oz	1.4 oz
33 lbs	840	6.3 oz	1.7 oz	6	2.1 oz	3.5 oz
44 lbs	1000	8.8 oz	2.1 oz	6	2.1 oz	3.5 oz
66 lbs	1400	15.8 oz	2.8 oz	8	3.5 oz	3.5 oz

Light Recipes for Underactive, Sterilized or Castrated Adult Dogs

Sterilized or castrated dogs, as well as those with lower activity levels, require a carefully balanced diet to maintain a healthy weight while still receiving all essential nutrients. These **light recipes** are designed to provide lean proteins, digestible carbohydrates, and fiber-rich vegetables, ensuring a well-rounded diet that supports overall well-being without excessive calories.

Maintaining an ideal weight is crucial for dogs with reduced energy needs, as excess weight can lead to joint strain, metabolic imbalances, and long-term health issues. These recipes prioritize **high-quality, lean proteins** such as chicken, turkey, cod, hake, beef, and pork, paired with **digestible grains** like rice, pasta, and bread. Additionally, **nutritious vegetables** like pumpkin, zucchini, spinach, and carrots provide fiber, vitamins, and minerals to promote digestion and satiety.

Each recipe includes **caloric adjustments** based on your dog's weight, making it easy to customize portions according to their individual needs. Whether your dog prefers poultry, fish, or red meat, this collection offers a variety of **tasty, nutritious, and easily digestible meals** tailored for a balanced, lighter diet.

By following these recipes, you can ensure that your dog receives **adequate nutrition** without excess calories, helping them stay fit, healthy, and happy while enjoying delicious, home-cooked meals.

Chicken & Veggie Bowl

A protein-rich meal with tender chicken, wholesome rice, and a mix of fresh vegetables.

This recipe is suitable for an underactive, sterilized or castrated **11-pound dog** with a daily caloric requirement of **290 calories**. Use the conversion tables to adjust the quantity based on your dog's weight.

Ingredients:
- 🐾 Chicken breast – 4.6 oz (cooked and shredded)
- 🐾 Rice – 0.7 oz (cooked)
- 🐾 Sunflower oil – 1 teaspoon
- 🐾 Vegetables (carrot, zucchini, and green beans) – 2.1 oz (finely chopped and lightly steamed)
- 🐾 Bread – 0.7 oz (crumbled)

Instructions:
1. Cook the chicken breast in water until fully cooked, then shred it into small pieces.
2. Cook the rice separately.
3. Lightly steam the carrot, zucchini, and green beans until soft.
4. In a bowl, mix the chicken, rice, and vegetables.
5. Drizzle with sunflower oil and stir well.
6. Crumble the bread and mix it in for added texture.
7. Let it cool before serving.

Conversion table

Dog's Weight	Calories	Chicken breast	Rice	Sunflower oil (tsp)	Vegetables	Bread
22 lbs	480	6.3 oz	1.4 oz	4	2.1 oz	0.7 oz
33 lbs	670	7.7 oz	1.4 oz	6	2.1 oz	1.7 oz
44 lbs	800	11.6 oz	2.1 oz	6	2.1 oz	1.7 oz
66 lbs	1100	15.8 oz	3.5 oz	6	3.5 oz	1.7 oz

Turkey & Pumpkin Comfort Meal

A soft, easy-to-digest dish perfect for dogs who enjoy mild and comforting flavors.

> This recipe is suitable for an underactive, sterilized or castrated **11-pound dog** with a daily caloric requirement of **290 calories**. Use the conversion tables to adjust the quantity based on your dog's weight.

Ingredients:
- 🐾 Turkey breast – 4.6 oz (boiled and shredded)
- 🐾 Pasta – 0.7 oz (cooked)
- 🐾 Corn oil – 1 teaspoon
- 🐾 Vegetables (pumpkin and spinach) – 2.1 oz (mashed and finely chopped)
- 🐾 Bread – 0.7 oz (cubed and softened in warm water)

Instructions:
1. Boil the turkey breast until fully cooked, then shred it.
2. Cook the pasta until soft.
3. Steam and mash the pumpkin, and finely chop the spinach.
4. In a bowl, mix the turkey, pasta, mashed pumpkin, and spinach.
5. Add corn oil and mix well.
6. Soak the bread in warm water and stir it in for a soft texture.
7. Let the meal cool before serving.

Conversion table

Dog's Weight	Calories	Turkey breast	Pasta	Corn oil (tsp)	Vegetables	Bread
22 lbs	480	6.3 oz	1.4 oz	4	2.1 oz	0.7 oz
33 lbs	670	7.7 oz	1.4 oz	6	2.1 oz	1.7 oz
44 lbs	800	11.6 oz	2.1 oz	6	2.1 oz	1.7 oz
66 lbs	1100	15.8 oz	3.5 oz	6	3.5 oz	1.7 oz

Cod & Carrot Medley

A light and digestible fish-based meal packed with healthy vegetables and rice.

> This recipe is suitable for an underactive, sterilized or castrated **11-pound dog** with a daily caloric requirement of **290 calories**. Use the conversion tables to adjust the quantity based on your dog's weight.

Ingredients:
- 🐾 Cod – 5.6 oz (boiled and flaked)
- 🐾 Rice – 1.1 oz (cooked)
- 🐾 Sunflower oil – 1 teaspoon
- 🐾 Vegetables (carrot, zucchini, and green beans) – 2.1 oz (finely chopped and lightly steamed)
- 🐾 Bread – 0.7 oz (crumbled)

Instructions:
1. Boil the cod until fully cooked, then flake it into small pieces.
2. Cook the rice separately according to package instructions.
3. Steam the carrot, zucchini, and green beans until soft.
4. In a bowl, mix the cod, rice, and vegetables.
5. Drizzle sunflower oil over the mixture and stir well.
6. Crumble the bread and mix it in for added texture.
7. Allow to cool before serving.

Conversion table

Dog's Weight	Calories	Cod	Rice	Sunflower oil (tsp)	Vegetables	Bread
22 lbs	480	9.1 oz	1.4 oz	4	2.1 oz	0.7 oz
33 lbs	670	9.1 oz	2.1 oz	6	2.1 oz	1.7 oz
44 lbs	800	13.4 oz	2.8 oz	6	2.1 oz	1.7 oz
66 lbs	1100	21.1 oz	3.8 oz	6	3.5 oz	1.7 oz

Hake & Pumpkin Power Bowl

A soft, easily digestible meal that's great for dogs with sensitive stomachs.

> This recipe is suitable for an underactive, sterilized or castrated **11-pound dog** with a daily caloric requirement of **290 calories**. Use the conversion tables to adjust the quantity based on your dog's weight.

Ingredients:
- 🐾 Hake – 5.6 oz (boiled and flaked)
- 🐾 Pasta – 1.1 oz (cooked)
- 🐾 Sunflower oil – 1 teaspoon
- 🐾 Vegetables (pumpkin and spinach) – 2.1 oz (mashed and finely chopped)
- 🐾 Bread – 0.7 oz (cubed and softened in warm water)

Instructions:
1. Boil the hake until fully cooked, then flake it into small pieces.
2. Cook the pasta until soft.
3. Steam and mash the pumpkin, and finely chop the spinach.
4. In a large bowl, mix the hake, pasta, mashed pumpkin, and spinach.
5. Add sunflower oil and stir well.
6. Soak the bread in warm water, then mix it in for a soft texture.
7. Let the dish cool before serving.

Conversion table

Dog's Weight	Calories	Hake	Pasta	Sunflower oil (tsp)	Vegetables	Bread
22 lbs	480	9.2 oz	1.4 oz	4	2.1 oz	0.7 oz
33 lbs	670	9.2 oz	2.1 oz	6	2.1 oz	1.7 oz
44 lbs	800	13.4 oz	2.8 oz	6	2.1 oz	1.7 oz
66 lbs	1100	21.2 oz	3.8 oz	6	3.5 oz	1.7 oz

Beef & Veggie Delight

A protein-rich and fiber-packed meal with lean beef, soft rice, and fresh vegetables.

This recipe is suitable for an underactive, sterilized or castrated **11-pound dog** with a daily caloric requirement of **290 calories**. Use the conversion tables to adjust the quantity based on your dog's weight.

Ingredients:
- Lean beef fillet – 3.9 oz (cooked and finely chopped)
- Rice – 0.4 oz (cooked)
- Sunflower oil – 1 teaspoon
- Vegetables (carrot, zucchini, and green beans) – 2.1 oz (finely chopped and lightly steamed)
- Bread – 0.7 oz (crumbled)

Instructions:
1. Cook the lean beef fillet in a pan with a little water until fully cooked, then chop it into small pieces.
2. Cook the rice separately.
3. Lightly steam the carrot, zucchini, and green beans until soft.
4. In a bowl, mix the cooked beef, rice, and vegetables.
5. Drizzle with sunflower oil and mix well.
6. Crumble the bread and stir it in for extra texture.
7. Let it cool before serving.

Conversion table

Dog's Weight	Calories	Lean beef	Rice	Sunflower oil (tsp)	Vegetables	Bread
22 lbs	480	6.7 oz	0.7 oz	2	2.1 oz	0.7 oz
33 lbs	670	7.7 oz	1 oz	4	2.1 oz	1.7 oz
44 lbs	800	10.5 oz	1.4 oz	4	2.1 oz	1.7 oz
66 lbs	1100	15.8 oz	1.7 oz	6	3.5 oz	1.7 oz

Pork & Pumpkin Comfort Bowl

A soft and easy-to-digest meal, great for dogs that love a mild and nourishing meal.

This recipe is suitable for an underactive, sterilized or castrated **11-pound dog** with a daily caloric requirement of **290 calories**. Use the conversion tables to adjust the quantity based on your dog's weight.

Ingredients:
- ❤️ Lean pork fillet – 3.9 oz (boiled and shredded)
- ❤️ Pasta – 0.4 oz (cooked)
- ❤️ Corn oil – 1 teaspoon
- ❤️ Vegetables (pumpkin and spinach) – 2.1 oz (mashed and finely chopped)
- ❤️ Bread – 0.7 oz (cubed and softened in warm water)

Instructions:
1. Boil the pork fillet until fully cooked, then shred it.
2. Cook the pasta until soft.
3. Steam and mash the pumpkin, and finely chop the spinach.
4. In a bowl, mix the pork, pasta, mashed pumpkin, and spinach.
5. Add corn oil and stir well.
6. Soak the bread in warm water, then mix it in for a soft texture.
7. Let the dish cool before serving.

Conversion table

Dog's Weight	Calories	Lean pork	Pasta	Corn oil (tsp)	Vegetables	Bread
22 lbs	480	6.7 oz	0.7 oz	2	2.1 oz	0.7 oz
33 lbs	670	7.7 oz	1 oz	4	2.1 oz	1.7 oz
44 lbs	800	10.5 oz	1.4 oz	4	2.1 oz	1.7 oz
66 lbs	1100	15.8 oz	1.7 oz	6	3.5 oz	1.7 oz

Hypoallergenic Recipes for Adult Dogs and Less Active, Sterilized or Castrated Dogs

Dogs with food sensitivities, allergies, or lower energy requirements need carefully curated meals that provide **balanced nutrition** while minimizing potential allergens and digestive issues. A well-planned diet is essential for **maintaining their overall health, preventing food-related discomfort**, and ensuring they receive all the necessary nutrients without unnecessary fillers or irritants.

If your dog has **known dietary sensitivities**, eliminating common allergens like chicken, beef, wheat, and dairy can help alleviate symptoms such as itchy skin, gastrointestinal upset, or chronic inflammation. On the other hand, if your dog has **reduced activity levels** due to sterilization, castration, or age, they require meals that support **healthy weight management** without excessive calories.

These hypoallergenic recipes focus on **gentle, easily digestible ingredients** that nourish your dog while reducing the risk of allergic reactions or digestive issues.

Two key ingredients play a crucial role in these meals:
- 🐾 **Rabbit Meat:** A **lean, high-quality protein source**, rabbit is an excellent alternative to common proteins like beef and chicken. It is rich in **essential amino acids** and beneficial for dogs prone to allergies or food sensitivities. Rabbit meat is also easy to digest, making it ideal for dogs with sensitive stomachs.
- 🐾 **Tapioca:** A **gluten-free, grain-free carbohydrate**, tapioca provides **a steady source of energy** without causing inflammation or triggering common intolerances. Unlike traditional grains such as wheat or corn,

tapioca is **highly digestible**, making it a safe and effective ingredient for hypoallergenic diets.

These recipes incorporate **nutrient-dense add-ins** such as sunflower oil, which provides healthy fats for skin and coat health, and pumpkin (when permitted), which supports digestion with its fiber content. For dogs still undergoing an **elimination diet or diagnostic phase**, a pumpkin-free version is available to further minimize potential allergens.

Every dog has different nutritional needs depending on their **size, weight, and activity level**. Each recipe is designed with **caloric adjustments** in mind, ensuring that portions can be tailored specifically for your dog's unique dietary requirements. This makes it easy to create **a sustainable meal plan** that maintains a healthy weight while still providing enough energy for daily activities.

For dogs that are **sterilized or castrated**, their metabolism may slow down, making it necessary to adjust calorie intake accordingly. A **lighter version** of each recipe is included, reducing fat and calorie content while maintaining the right balance of protein and essential nutrients. This approach helps prevent **unwanted weight gain** and supports **long-term well-being** without compromising on taste or satiety.

These carefully crafted meals offer a **simple, effective, and nutritious** way to cater to dogs with specific dietary needs. Whether you're managing **food allergies, digestive sensitivities, or post-sterilization weight control**, these recipes provide a **wholesome, homemade solution** that ensures your dog thrives.

Rabbit & Pumpkin Delight

A lean and easily digestible meal packed with protein from rabbit meat and energy-boosting tapioca.

This recipe is suitable for a hypoallergenic, active, **11-pound dog** with a daily caloric requirement of **370 calories**. Use the conversion tables to adjust the quantity based on your dog's weight, and activity level. If your dog is sterilized or castrated, follow the light version based on its weight.

Ingredients:
- 🐾 Rabbit meat – 2.8 oz (cooked and shredded)
- 🐾 Tapioca – 1.8 oz (cooked)
- 🐾 Sunflower oil – 2 teaspoons
- 🐾 Pumpkin – 2.1 oz (steamed and mashed) (Only when permitted)

Instructions:
1. Cook the rabbit meat in water until fully cooked, then shred it into small pieces.
2. Cook the tapioca separately according to instructions until soft.
3. Steam the pumpkin and mash it (omit if still in the diagnostic phase).
4. In a bowl, mix the rabbit, tapioca, and pumpkin.
5. Drizzle with sunflower oil and stir well.
6. Let the dish cool before serving.

Conversion table

Dog's Weight	Calories	Rabbit meat	Tapioca	Sunflower oil (tsp)	Pumpkin
22 lbs	600	4.2 oz	2.8 oz	4	2.1 oz
33 lbs	840	5.6 oz	3.8 oz	6	2.1 oz
44 lbs	1000	7.4 oz	4.5 oz	6	3.5 oz
66 lbs	1400	10.5 oz	7 oz	8	3.5 oz

Light version

Dog's Weight	Calories	Rabbit meat	Tapioca	Sunflower oil (tsp)	Pumpkin
11 lbs	290	2.1	1.41	1	2.1 oz
22 lbs	480	3.5 oz	2.1 oz	4	2.1 oz
33 lbs	670	5 oz	2.8 oz	6	2.1 oz
44 lbs	800	6 oz	4.2 oz	4	2.1 oz
66 lbs	1100	8.8 oz	5.2 oz	4	3.5 oz

Rabbit & Tapioca Energy Boost (Pumpkin-Free for Diagnostic Period)

A simple, gentle, and nutritious dish designed for dogs undergoing dietary adjustments.

This recipe is suitable for a hypoallergenic, active, **11-pound dog** with a daily caloric requirement of **370 calories**. Use the conversion tables to adjust the quantity based on your dog's weight, and activity level. If your dog is sterilized or castrated, follow the light version based on its weight.

Ingredients:
- 🐾 Rabbit meat – 2.8 oz (boiled and shredded)
- 🐾 Tapioca – 1.8 oz (cooked)
- 🐾 Sunflower oil – 2 teaspoons

Instructions:
1. Boil the rabbit meat until fully cooked, then shred it into small, digestible pieces.
2. Cook the tapioca separately until soft.
3. In a bowl, combine the rabbit meat and tapioca.
4. Drizzle with sunflower oil and stir to blend evenly.
5. Allow to cool before serving.

Conversion table

Dog's Weight	Calories	Rabbit meat	Tapioca	Sunflower oil (tsp)
22 lbs	600	4.2 oz	2.82 oz	4
33 lbs	840	5.6 oz	3.88 oz	6
44 lbs	1000	7.4 oz	4.58 oz	6
66 lbs	1400	10.5 oz	7.05 oz	8

Light version

Dog's Weight	Calories	Rabbit meat	Tapioca	Sunflower oil (tsp)
11 lbs	290	2.1	1.4	1
22 lbs	480	3.5 oz	2.1 oz	4
33 lbs	670	4.9 oz	2.8 oz	6
44 lbs	800	6 oz	4.2 oz	4
66 lbs	1100	8.8 oz	5.2 oz	4

Grain-Free Recipes for Active Adult Dogs and Less Active, Sterilized or Castrated Dogs

A grain-free diet can be beneficial for dogs with **food sensitivities, digestive issues, or specific dietary needs**, ensuring they receive **wholesome, nutrient-dense meals** without common allergens like wheat, rice, or corn. These grain-free recipes provide a **balanced combination of proteins, healthy fats, fiber-rich vegetables, and natural carbohydrates**, making them suitable for both **highly active dogs and those with lower energy requirements due to sterilization or castration**.

Why Choose Grain-Free Meals for Your Dog?

- 🐾 **Easier Digestion** – Many dogs experience sensitivities to grains, leading to issues like bloating, gas, or itchy skin. Substituting grains with **easily digestible alternatives**, such as **potatoes and pumpkin**, helps promote **better gut health and nutrient absorption**.
- 🐾 **Sustained Energy Levels** – Active dogs need **complex carbohydrates** to fuel their daily activities. **Potatoes and vegetables** provide a **slow release of energy**, helping maintain **stamina and endurance** throughout the day.
- 🐾 **Weight Management for Less Active or Sterilized Dogs** – Dogs that have undergone **sterilization or castration** tend to have **lower metabolic rates**, making them more prone to **weight gain**. The **light versions** of these recipes provide **lower-calorie, portion-controlled meals** while still ensuring complete nutrition.
- 🐾 **Anti-Inflammatory Benefits** – Ingredients such as **pumpkin, spinach, and apples** contain **antioxidants and fiber**, which support **immune function, reduce inflammation, and promote digestive health**.

Each recipe includes **adjustable portion sizes**, allowing you to modify meal servings **based on your dog's weight and activity level**. The **standard version** is designed for **energetic dogs** that require **higher caloric intake**, while the **light version** is perfect for **dogs with lower energy demands**, ensuring they maintain **a healthy weight** without feeling hungry or deprived.

By eliminating grains and focusing on **high-quality proteins, healthy fats, and fiber-rich vegetables**, these recipes provide a **well-rounded and nourishing diet** for your dog. Whether your dog is **an active explorer** or **a less energetic companion**, these grain-free meals support **sustained energy, digestive health, and long-term wellness**.

With **easy-to-follow cooking methods** and **simple, natural ingredients**, these recipes ensure your dog gets the **best possible nutrition in every meal**—fueling their adventures or helping them maintain a balanced weight with **delicious, homemade grain-free food**.

Pork & Veggie Power Bowl

A hearty, fiber-rich meal with lean pork, soft potatoes, and a mix of colorful vegetables.

This grain-free recipe is suitable for an active, sterilized or castrated **11-pound dog** with a daily caloric requirement of **370 calories**. Use the conversion tables to adjust the quantity based on your dog's weight, and activity level. If your dog is sterilized or castrated, follow the light version based on its weight.

Ingredients:
- 🐾 Pork loin – 3.5 oz (cooked and shredded)
- 🐾 Potatoes – 5.3 oz (boiled and mashed)
- 🐾 Sunflower oil – 2 teaspoons
- 🐾 Vegetables (carrot, zucchini, and green beans) – 2.1 oz (finely chopped and lightly steamed)
- 🐾 Apple – 1.8 oz (finely chopped)

Instructions:
1. Cook the pork loin in water until fully cooked, then shred it into small, manageable pieces.
2. Peel and boil the potatoes until soft, then mash them.
3. Steam the carrot, zucchini, and green beans until tender.
4. Finely chop the apple into small pieces.
5. In a large bowl, mix the pork, mashed potatoes, and vegetables.
6. Add the apple for a touch of natural sweetness.
7. Drizzle with sunflower oil and mix everything well.
8. Allow to cool before serving.

Conversion table

Dog's Weight	Calories	Pork loin	Potatoes	Sunflower oil (tsp)	Vegetables	Apple
22 lbs	600	7 oz	9.8 oz	2	2.1 oz	1.7 oz
33 lbs	840	8.8 oz	14 oz	4	2.1 oz	3.5 oz
44 lbs	1000	12 oz	15.7 oz	4	2.1 oz	3.5 oz
66 lbs	1400	17 oz	19 oz	6	2.1 oz	5.3 oz

Light version

Dog's Weight	Calories	Pork loin	Potatoes	Sunflower oil (tsp)	Vegetables	Apple
11 lbs	290	3.5 oz	2.5 oz	1	2.1 oz	1.7 oz
22 lbs	480	7 oz	6 oz	1	2.1 oz	1.7 oz
33 lbs	670	8.8 oz	9.1 oz	2	2.1 oz	3.5 oz
44 lbs	800	12.4 oz	9.1 oz	2	2.1 oz	3.5 oz
66 lbs	1100	17.6 oz	9.1 oz	4	2.1 oz	5.3 oz

Pork & Pumpkin Comfort Meal

A soft and digestible meal with lean pork, pumpkin, and a hint of apple for extra flavor.

This grain-free recipe is suitable for an active, sterilized or castrated **11-pound dog** with a daily caloric requirement of **370 calories**. Use the conversion tables to adjust the quantity based on your dog's weight, and activity level. If your dog is sterilized or castrated, follow the light version based on its weight.

Ingredients:
- 🐾 Pork loin – 3.5 oz (boiled and shredded)
- 🐾 Potatoes – 5.3 oz (boiled and mashed)
- 🐾 Sunflower oil – 2 teaspoons
- 🐾 Vegetables (pumpkin and spinach) – 2.1 oz (steamed and mashed)
- 🐾 Apple – 1.8 oz (grated)

Instructions:
1. Boil the pork loin until fully cooked, then shred it into small pieces.
2. Peel and boil the potatoes until soft, then mash them.
3. Steam and mash the pumpkin, and finely chop the spinach.
4. Grate the apple for a smoother texture.
5. In a bowl, mix the pork, mashed potatoes, mashed pumpkin, and spinach.
6. Add the grated apple and stir well.
7. Drizzle with sunflower oil and mix everything together.
8. Let it cool before serving.

Conversion table

Dog's Weight	Calories	Pork loin	Potatoes	Sunflower oil (tsp)	Vegetables	Apple
22 lbs	600	7 oz	9.8 oz	2	2.1 oz	1.7 oz
33 lbs	840	8.8 oz	14 oz	4	2.1 oz	3.5 oz
44 lbs	1000	12 oz	15.8 oz	4	2.1 oz	3.5 oz
66 lbs	1400	18 oz	19 oz	6	2.1 oz	5.3 oz

Light version

Dog's Weight	Calories	Pork loin	Potatoes	Sunflower oil (tsp)	Vegetables	Apple
11 lbs	290	3.5 oz	2.5 oz	1	2.1 oz	1.7 oz
22 lbs	480	7 oz	6 oz	1	2.1 oz	1.7 oz
33 lbs	670	8.8 oz	9.1 oz	2	2.1 oz	3.5 oz
44 lbs	800	12.3 oz	9.1 oz	2	2.1 oz	3.5 oz
66 lbs	1100	17.63oz	9.1 oz	4	2.1 oz	5.3 oz

BARF Recipes for Active Adult Dogs and Less Active, Sterilized or Castrated Dogs

The Biologically Appropriate Raw Food (BARF) diet is designed to provide dogs with nutrient-dense, whole-food meals that mimic their natural diet in the wild. These BARF-inspired cooked recipes offer the benefits of a high-protein, minimally processed diet, while ensuring safety and digestibility for all dogs, including those with reduced activity levels due to sterilization or castration.

By incorporating fresh, natural ingredients, these recipes provide a balanced combination of proteins, organ meats, vegetables, and healthy fats, ensuring optimal muscle development, immune function, and digestive health.

Benefits of the BARF diet
- 🐾 **High-Quality Proteins for Muscle Strength & Energy.** These recipes use lean beef and nutrient-rich organ meats, which are excellent sources of essential amino acids, iron, and B vitamins to support muscle growth, stamina, and cell function.
- 🐾 **Organ Meats for Vital Nutrients.** Organ meats such as heart, spleen, kidneys, lungs, and liver are nutritional powerhouses, providing vitamins A, D, and E, along with minerals like zinc, copper, and selenium, which support metabolism, immune function, and joint health.
- 🐾 **Wholesome Carbohydrates for Energy & Satiety.** Instead of grains, these recipes feature potatoes and pumpkin, which offer digestible energy sources while being gentle on the stomach. Potatoes provide fiber and potassium, while pumpkin adds beta-carotene and antioxidants, supporting digestive health and skin vitality.

- 🐾 **Healthy Fats for Skin, Coat & Brain Health.** Sunflower oil, a key ingredient in these meals, is rich in omega-6 fatty acids, which help maintain a healthy coat, reduce inflammation, and promote cognitive function.
- 🐾 **Fruits & Vegetables for Digestive Support & Immunity.** These recipes incorporate carrot, zucchini, green beans, spinach, chard, and apples, providing fiber, vitamins, and antioxidants to support gut health, heart function, and disease prevention. Apples also add a touch of natural sweetness, making meals more palatable for picky eaters.

Every dog's caloric and macronutrient needs vary, depending on their size, energy levels, and metabolism.

- 🐾 For active adult dogs, these recipes provide higher protein and calorie content to fuel muscle repair, endurance, and energy demands.
- 🐾 For sterilized or less active dogs, the light version of each recipe reduces calories while maintaining the same essential nutrients, ensuring they stay fit without excessive weight gain.

Each recipe includes portion conversion tables, making it easy to customize meal sizes based on your dog's weight and activity level.

Beef & Organ Meat Power Bowl

A high-protein, energy-packed meal with lean beef, nutrient-rich organ meats, and wholesome potatoes.

This BARF recipe is suitable for an active, sterilized or castrated **11-pound dog** with a daily caloric requirement of **370 calories**. Use the conversion tables to adjust the quantity based on your dog's weight, and activity level. If your dog is sterilized or castrated, follow the light version based on its weight.

Ingredients:
- 🐾 Lean beef (no visible fat) – 2.5 oz (cooked and chopped)
- 🐾 Organ meats (heart, spleen, kidneys, lungs, liver) – 1.1 oz (boiled and chopped)
- 🐾 Potatoes – 7 oz (boiled and mashed)
- 🐾 Sunflower oil – 2 teaspoons
- 🐾 Vegetables (carrot, zucchini, and green beans) – 2.1 oz (lightly steamed and chopped)
- 🐾 Apple – 1.8 oz (finely chopped)

Instructions:
1. Boil the lean beef and organ meats until fully cooked, then chop them into small pieces.
2. Peel and boil the potatoes until soft, then mash them.
3. Steam the carrot, zucchini, and green beans until tender.
4. Chop the apple into small pieces.
5. In a large bowl, mix the beef, organ meats, mashed potatoes, and vegetables.
6. Add the apple for a natural sweetness.
7. Drizzle with sunflower oil and stir well.
8. Let the meal cool before serving.

Conversion table

Dog's Weight	Calories	Lean beef	Organ meats	Potatoes	Sunflower oil (tsp)	Vegetables	Apple
22 lbs	600	5 oz	1.7 oz	9.8 oz	2	2.1 oz	1.7 oz
33 lbs	840	9 oz	1.7 oz	14 oz	4	2.1 oz	1.7 oz
44 lbs	1000	9 oz	3.5 oz	16.2 oz	4	2.1 oz	3.5 oz
66 lbs	1400	12 oz	5.3 oz	21.1 oz	6	2.1 oz	5.3 oz

Light version

Dog's Weight	Calories	Lean beef	Organ meats	Potatoes	Sunflower oil (tsp)	Vegetables	Apple
11 lbs	290	2.5 oz	1 oz	3.2 oz	2	2.11 oz	1.7 oz
22 lbs	480	5.2 oz	1.7 oz	6 oz	1	2.11 oz	1.7 oz
33 lbs	670	8.8 oz	1.7 oz	7 oz	2	2.11 oz	3.5 oz
44 lbs	800	8.8 oz	3.5 oz	9.8 oz	2	2.11 oz	3.5 oz
66 lbs	1100	12.4 oz	5.3 oz	10.5 oz	4	2.11 oz	5.3 oz

Hearty Pumpkin & Beef Mash

A soft, gentle, and highly digestible dish, perfect for dogs needing extra nutrients.

> This BARF recipe is suitable for an active, sterilized or castrated **11-pound dog** with a daily caloric requirement of **370 calories**. Use the conversion tables to adjust the quantity based on your dog's weight, and activity level. If your dog is sterilized or castrated, follow the light version based on its weight.

Ingredients:
- 🐾 Lean beef (no visible fat) – 2.5 oz (boiled and shredded)
- 🐾 Organ meats (heart, spleen, kidneys, lungs, liver) – 1.1 oz (boiled and finely chopped)
- 🐾 Potatoes – 7 oz (boiled and mashed)
- 🐾 Sunflower oil – 2 teaspoons
- 🐾 Vegetables (pumpkin and spinach) – 2.1 oz (steamed and mashed)
- 🐾 Apple – 1.8 oz (grated)

Instructions:
1. Boil the lean beef and organ meats until fully cooked, then shred and chop them.
2. Peel and boil the potatoes until soft, then mash them.
3. Steam and mash the pumpkin, and finely chop the spinach.
4. Grate the apple for a smoother texture.
5. In a bowl, mix the beef, organ meats, mashed potatoes, mashed pumpkin, and spinach.
6. Add the grated apple for extra fiber.
7. Drizzle with sunflower oil and mix everything together.
8. Allow to cool before serving.

Conversion table

Dog's Weight	Calories	Lean beef	Organ meats	Potatoes	Sunflower oil (tsp)	Vegetables	Apple
22 lbs	600	5.2 oz	1.7 oz	9.8 oz	2	2.11 oz	1.7 oz
33 lbs	840	8.8 oz	1.7 oz	14 oz	4	2.11 oz	1.7 oz
44 lbs	1000	8.8 oz	3.5 oz	16.2 oz	4	2.11 oz	3.5 oz
66 lbs	1400	12.3 oz	5.3 oz	21.1 oz	6	2.11 oz	5.3 oz

Light version

Dog's Weight	Calories	Lean beef	Organ meats	Potatoes	Sunflower oil (tsp)	Vegetables	Apple
11 lbs	290	2.5 oz	1 oz	3.17 oz	2	2.11 oz	1.7 oz
22 lbs	480	5.3 oz	1.7 oz	6 oz	1	2.11 oz	1.7 oz
33 lbs	670	8.8 oz	1.7 oz	7 oz	2	2.11 oz	3.5 oz
44 lbs	800	8.8 oz	3.5 oz	9.8 oz	2	2.11 oz	3.5 oz
66 lbs	1100	12.3 oz	5.3 oz	10.6 oz	4	2.11 oz	5.3 oz

Beef & Veggie Stew

A warm, comforting stew loaded with beef, organ meats, vegetables, and potatoes.

This BARF recipe is suitable for an active, sterilized or castrated **11-pound dog** with a daily caloric requirement of **370 calories**. Use the conversion tables to adjust the quantity based on your dog's weight, and activity level. If your dog is sterilized or castrated, follow the light version based on its weight.

Ingredients:
- Lean beef (no visible fat) – 2.5 oz (cubed)
- Organ meats (heart, spleen, kidneys, lungs, liver) – 1.1 oz (chopped)
- Potatoes – 7 oz (cubed)
- Sunflower oil – 2 teaspoons
- Vegetables (carrot, chard, and green beans) – 2.1 oz (chopped)
- Apple – 1.8 oz (chopped)
- Water – 1/2 cup (optional, for stew consistency)

Instructions:
1. In a pot, add cubed beef, organ meats, and potatoes, and cover with water.
2. Bring to a boil, then simmer until the potatoes are soft and the meats are fully cooked.
3. Add the chopped vegetables and simmer for an additional 5 minutes.
4. Remove from heat, let cool slightly, and stir in the sunflower oil.
5. Chop the apple into small pieces and mix it in.
6. Serve slightly warm or at room temperature.

Conversion table

Dog's Weight	Calories	Lean beef	Organ meats	Potatoes	Sunflower oil (tsp)	Vegetables	Apple	Water
22 lbs	600	5.3 oz	1.7 oz	9.8 oz	2	2.1 oz	1.7 oz	1/2 cup
33 lbs	840	8.8 oz	1.7 oz	14 oz	4	2.1 oz	1.7 oz	1/2 cup
44 lbs	1000	8.8 oz	3.5 oz	16.2 oz	4	2.1 oz	3.5 oz	1/2 cup
66 lbs	1400	12.3 oz	5.3 oz	21.1 oz	6	2.11 oz	5.3 oz	1/2 cup

Light version

Dog's Weight	Calories	Lean beef	Organ meats	Potatoes	Sunflower oil (tsp)	Vegetables	Apple	Water
11 lbs	290	2.5 oz	1 oz	3.2 oz	2	2.1 oz	1.7 oz	1/2 cup
22 lbs	480	5.3 oz	1.7 oz	6 oz	1	2.1 oz	1.7 oz	1/2 cup
33 lbs	670	8.8 oz	1.7 oz	7 oz	2	2.1 oz	3.5 oz	1/2 cup
44 lbs	800	8.8 oz	3.5 oz	9.8 oz	2	2.1 oz	3.5 oz	1/2 cup
66 lbs	1100	12.4 oz	5.3 oz	10.5 oz	4	2.1 oz	5.3 oz	1/2 cup

Vegetarian Recipes for Active Adult Dogs and Less Active, Sterilized or Castrated Dogs

A well-balanced **vegetarian diet** can provide **complete nutrition** for dogs when carefully formulated with **high-quality proteins, healthy fats, and fiber-rich vegetables**. These recipes are designed to meet the needs of both **active adult dogs** and **less active, sterilized, or castrated dogs**, ensuring they receive all the essential nutrients without meat-based ingredients.

While dogs are **omnivores** and can thrive on a vegetarian diet, it is important to ensure that their meals contain **sufficient protein, essential fatty acids, and digestible carbohydrates**. These carefully curated **vegetarian recipes** offer a variety of flavors and textures while delivering **energy, muscle support, and digestive health benefits**.

Why Choose a Vegetarian Diet for Your Dog?
- 🐾 **Gentle on Digestion** – These meals incorporate **easy-to-digest proteins** like **eggs and yogurt**, along with **soft vegetables and couscous**, making them ideal for dogs with **sensitive stomachs** or **food allergies**.
- 🐾 **High-Quality Protein Sources** – **Eggs and egg whites** provide a **complete amino acid profile**, essential for **muscle maintenance, immune function, and overall energy**.
- 🐾 **Healthy Fats for Skin & Coat Health** – **Sunflower oil** is rich in **omega-6 fatty acids**, which support **skin hydration, coat shine, and joint function**.
- 🐾 **Calcium & Probiotics for Gut Health** – **Low-fat yogurt and Parmesan cheese** provide **calcium for strong bones** and **probiotics to support digestion and gut health**.

- 🐾 **Fiber & Antioxidants from Vegetables & Fruits** – Vegetables like **spinach, chard, pumpkin, zucchini, and carrots** add **fiber, vitamins, and antioxidants** to support **immune function and healthy digestion**. Apples and pumpkin offer a **natural sweetness** while boosting fiber intake.
- 🐾 **Balanced Energy for Active & Less Active Dogs** – **Couscous and vegetables** provide a steady release of **digestible carbohydrates**, helping maintain **energy levels** for active dogs while offering **lower-calorie options for dogs with reduced activity levels**.

By choosing these **homemade vegetarian recipes**, you can ensure your dog receives **a well-rounded diet** with **essential proteins, vitamins, and minerals** while enjoying **variety and flavorful meals**. Whether your dog is **highly active** or **requires a lower-calorie meal plan**, these recipes offer a **safe, balanced, and satisfying approach to vegetarian nutrition**.

With **simple, whole-food ingredients**, these meals help your dog **maintain energy, digestive health, and overall well-being**, ensuring a **happy, healthy life on a vegetarian diet**!

Creamy Egg & Pumpkin Mash

A smooth and creamy dish with the mild sweetness of pumpkin.

This vegetarian recipe is suitable for an active, sterilized or castrated **11-pound dog** with a daily caloric requirement of **370 calories**. Use the conversion tables to adjust the quantity based on your dog's weight, and activity level. If your dog is sterilized or castrated, follow the light version based on its weight.

Ingredients:
- Medium chicken egg – 1.9 oz (boiled and mashed)
- Egg whites – 2.6 oz (boiled and chopped)
- Couscous – 1.8 oz (cooked)
- Sunflower oil – 2 teaspoons
- Vegetables (pumpkin and spinach) – 1.1 oz (steamed and mashed)
- Low-fat yogurt – 4.4 oz (mixed in for creaminess)

Instructions:
1. Cook the couscous separately.
2. Boil the egg and egg whites, then mash them.
3. Steam and mash the pumpkin, and finely chop the spinach.
4. In a bowl, combine the mashed egg, egg whites, couscous, pumpkin, and spinach.
5. Drizzle with sunflower oil and mix well.
6. Stir in the low-fat yogurt for a creamy texture.
7. Serve slightly warm or at room temperature.

Conversion table

Dog's Weight	Calories	Chicken egg	Egg whites	Couscous	Sunflower oil (tsp)	Vegetables	Low-fat yogurt
22 lbs	600	1	5	3.1 oz	4	1 oz	4.5 oz

Light version

Dog's Weight	Calories	Chicken egg	Egg whites	Couscous	Sunflower oil (tsp)	Vegetables	Low-fat yogurt
11 lbs	290	1	2	1.2 oz	1	1 oz	4.5 oz
22 lbs	480	1	5	2.2 oz	2	1 oz	4.5 oz

Egg & Yogurt Protein Bowl

A soft, digestible, and nutrient-packed meal with a creamy yogurt base.

This vegetarian recipe is suitable for an active, sterilized or castrated **11-pound dog** with a daily caloric requirement of **370 calories**. Use the conversion tables to adjust the quantity based on your dog's weight, and activity level. If your dog is sterilized or castrated, follow the light version based on its weight.

Ingredients:
- Medium chicken egg – 1.9 oz (scrambled)
- Egg whites – 2.6 oz (scrambled)
- Couscous – 1.8 oz (cooked)
- Sunflower oil – 2 teaspoons
- Vegetables (green beans and chard) – 1.1 oz (lightly steamed and chopped)
- Low-fat yogurt – 4.4 oz (as a base)

Instructions:
1. Cook the couscous and let it cool slightly.
2. Lightly scramble the egg and egg whites in a pan.
3. Steam the green beans and chard, then chop finely.
4. In a bowl, spread the low-fat yogurt as a base.
5. Add the cooked couscous, scrambled eggs, and vegetables on top.
6. Drizzle with sunflower oil and mix slightly before serving.

Conversion table

Dog's Weight	Calories	Chicken egg	Egg whites	Couscous	Sunflower oil (tsp)	Vegetables	Low-fat yogurt
22 lbs	600	1	5	3.1 oz	4	1 oz	4.5 oz

Light version

Dog's Weight	Calories	Chicken egg	Egg whites	Couscous	Sunflower oil (tsp)	Vegetables	Low-fat yogurt
11 lbs	290	1	2	1.2 oz	1	1 oz	4.5 oz
22 lbs	480	1	5	2.2 oz	2	1 oz	4.5 oz

Fluffy Egg & Veggie Muffins

This vegetarian recipe is suitable for an active, sterilized or castrated **33-pound dog** with a daily caloric requirement of **840 calories**. Use the conversion tables to adjust the quantity based on your dog's weight, and activity level. If your dog is sterilized or castrated, follow the light version based on its weight.

Ingredients:
- 🐾 Medium chicken egg – 1.9 oz (1 egg)
- 🐾 Egg whites – 9.1 oz (7 egg whites)
- 🐾 Couscous – 3.9 oz (cooked)
- 🐾 Sunflower oil – 6 teaspoons
- 🐾 Parmesan cheese – 0.7 oz (grated)
- 🐾 Vegetables (carrot and zucchini) – 2.1 oz (grated)
- 🐾 Low-fat yogurt – 4.4 oz (for serving)

Instructions:
1. Preheat the oven to 350°F (175°C) and grease a muffin tin with the oil.
2. In a bowl, whisk together the egg and egg whites until fluffy.
3. Stir in the cooked couscous, grated carrot, zucchini, and Parmesan cheese.
4. Bake for 12-15 minutes or until firm and golden.
5. Let cool before serving with a spoonful of yogurt on the side.

Conversion table

Dog's Weight	Calories	Egg	Egg whites	Couscous	Sunflower oil (tsp)	Parmesan cheese	Vegetables	Low-fat yogurt
44 lbs	1000	1	7	4.7 oz	8	1 oz	2.1 oz	4.4 oz
66 lbs	1400	1	8	7 oz	8	2.4 oz	3.5 oz	4.4 oz

Light version

Dog's Weight	Calories	Egg	Egg whites	Couscous	Sunflower oil (tsp)	Parmesan cheese	Vegetables	Low-fat yogurt
44 lbs	800	1	7	3.1 oz	6	1 oz	2.1 oz	4.4 oz
66 lbs	1100	1	8	4.4 oz	6	2.4 oz	3.5 oz	4.4 oz

Frozen Yogurt & Egg Bites

This vegetarian recipe is suitable for an active, sterilized or castrated **33-pound dog** with a daily caloric requirement of **840 calories**. Use the conversion tables to adjust the quantity based on your dog's weight, and activity level. If your dog is sterilized or castrated, follow the light version based on its weight.

Ingredients:
- 🐾 Medium chicken egg – 1.9 oz (1 egg, boiled and mashed)
- 🐾 Egg whites – 9.1 oz (boiled and mashed)
- 🐾 Couscous – 3.9 oz (cooked and cooled)
- 🐾 Sunflower oil – 6 teaspoons
- 🐾 Parmesan cheese – 0.7 oz (grated)
- 🐾 Vegetables (pumpkin, mashed) – 2.1 oz
- 🐾 Low-fat yogurt – 4.4 oz

Instructions:
1. Boil the egg and egg whites, then mash them well.
2. Mix the cooked couscous, mashed pumpkin, grated Parmesan, and oil.
3. Add the low-fat yogurt and stir until well combined.
4. Spoon the mixture into silicone ice cube trays or molds.
5. Freeze for at least 3 hours, or until solid.
6. Serve as a cold, protein-packed treat!

Conversion table

Dog's Weight	Calories	Egg	Egg whites	Couscous	Sunflower oil (tsp)	Parmesan cheese	Vegetables	Low-fat yogurt
44 lbs	1000	1	7	4.7 oz	8	1 oz	2.11 oz	4.4 oz
66 lbs	1400	1	8	7 oz	8	2.4 oz	3.5 oz	4.4 oz

Light version

Dog's Weight	Calories	Egg	Egg whites	Couscous	Sunflower oil (tsp)	Parmesan cheese	Vegetables	Low-fat yogurt
44 lbs	800	1	7	3.1 oz	6	1 oz	2.1 oz	4.4 oz
66 lbs	1100	1	8	4.4 oz	6	2.4 oz	3.5 oz	4.4 oz

Cheesy Egg Pancakes

A delicious flat, omelet-like meal that's packed with protein and flavor.

This vegetarian recipe is suitable for an active, sterilized or castrated **33-pound dog** with a daily caloric requirement of **840 calories**. Use the conversion tables to adjust the quantity based on your dog's weight, and activity level. If your dog is sterilized or castrated, follow the light version based on its weight.

Ingredients:
- Medium chicken egg – 1.9 oz (1 egg)
- Egg whites – 9.1 oz (7 egg whites)
- Couscous – 3.9 oz (cooked)
- Sunflower oil – 6 teaspoons
- Parmesan cheese – 0.7 oz (grated)
- Vegetables (spinach and chard) – 2.1 oz (finely chopped)
- Low-fat yogurt – 4.4 oz (for serving)

Instructions:
1. In a bowl, whisk together the egg and egg whites.
2. Stir in the cooked couscous, grated Parmesan cheese, and finely chopped vegetables.
3. Heat a non-stick pan with a small amount of sunflower oil over low-medium heat.
4. Pour the batter into the pan, spreading it evenly like a pancake.
5. Cook for 3-4 minutes per side, flipping carefully.
6. Let cool before cutting into strips and serving with yogurt on the side.

Conversion table

Dog's Weight	Calories	Egg	Egg whites	Couscous	Sunflower oil (tsp)	Parmesan cheese	Vegetables	Low-fat yogurt
44 lbs	1000	1	7	4.7 oz	8	1 oz	2.1 oz	4.4 oz
66 lbs	1400	1	8	7 oz	8	2.4 oz	3.5 oz	4.4 oz

Light version

Dog's Weight	Calories	Egg	Egg whites	Couscous	Sunflower oil (tsp)	Parmesan cheese	Vegetables	Low-fat yogurt
44 lbs	800	1	7	3.1 oz	6	1 oz	2.1 oz	4.4 oz
66 lbs	1100	1	8	4.4 oz	6	2.4 oz	3.5 oz	4.4 oz

Chapter 10: Homemade Treats and Snacks

Homemade dog treats are a fantastic way to supplement your dog's diet with healthy, nutritious, and preservative-free snacks. Not only do they provide a great way to reward good behavior, but they can also serve functional roles such as promoting dental health, aiding digestion, or supporting joint care. In this chapter, we'll explore a variety of homemade treat recipes, discuss the role of treats in a balanced diet, and provide special recipes catering to different health needs.

The Role of Treats in a Balanced Diet

While treats are an enjoyable addition to your dog's meals, they should never replace a balanced, complete diet. The key to incorporating treats responsibly is moderation—ensuring they **do not exceed 10% of your dog's daily caloric intake**. Excessive treats can lead to unwanted weight gain, digestive issues, and nutritional imbalances that may affect overall health.

It's also important to be mindful of the ingredients in the treats you offer. Many commercial options contain unnecessary fillers, artificial flavors, and chemical preservatives, which may not provide any real nutritional value and could even be harmful in the long run. Choosing to make homemade treats gives you full control over the ingredients, allowing you to prioritize high-quality, nutrient-dense components. This way, you can ensure your dog receives wholesome, natural snacks that complement their diet rather than detract from it.

Homemade Dog Treat Recipes

Below are a few easy-to-make dog treat recipes that your pup will love. Each recipe uses wholesome, dog-safe ingredients that provide both flavor and nutritional benefits.

Peanut Butter and Oatmeal Cookies

Best for: General snacking, high-energy dogs

Ingredients:
- 1 cup oat flour
- ½ cup rolled oats
- ½ cup unsweetened peanut butter (xylitol-free)
- 1 ripe banana, mashed
- 1 egg
- ¼ cup water (if needed for consistency)

Instructions:
1. Preheat oven to 350°F (175°C).
2. Mix all ingredients in a bowl until a dough forms.
3. Roll out and cut into shapes or drop spoonful onto a baking sheet.
4. Bake for 12–15 minutes or until golden brown.
5. Let cool before serving.

Sweet Potato Chews

Best for: Dental health, long-lasting chew

Ingredients:
- 1 large, sweet potato, sliced into thin rounds

Instructions:
1. Preheat oven to 250°F (120°C).
2. Arrange sweet potato slices on a baking sheet lined with parchment paper.
3. Bake for 2–3 hours, flipping halfway through.

4. Let cool completely; the chews will harden as they cool.
5. Store in an airtight container for up to two weeks.

Frozen Yogurt and Blueberry Bites

Best for: Summertime cool-down, antioxidant boost

Ingredients:
- 🐾 1 cup plain Greek yogurt
- 🐾 ½ cup fresh or frozen blueberries
- 🐾 1 tablespoon honey (optional)

Instructions:
1. Blend yogurt, blueberries, and honey until smooth.
2. Pour into silicone molds or ice cube trays.
3. Freeze for 3–4 hours or until solid.
4. Serve as a refreshing treat on hot days.

Hypoallergenic Pumpkin Biscuits

Best for: Dogs with food sensitivities or allergies

Ingredients:
- 🐾 1 cup chickpea flour
- 🐾 ½ cup pumpkin puree
- 🐾 1 tablespoon coconut oil
- 🐾 1 teaspoon cinnamon

Instructions:
1. Preheat oven to 325°F (165°C).
2. Mix all ingredients into a dough.
3. Roll out and cut into small shapes.
4. Bake for 20 minutes, flipping halfway.
5. Allow to cool before serving.

Joint-Boosting Turmeric Treats

Best for: Senior dogs, joint health support

Ingredients:
- 🐾 1 ½ cups oat flour
- 🐾 ½ cup pumpkin puree
- 🐾 1 tablespoon turmeric powder
- 🐾 ½ teaspoon black pepper (enhances turmeric absorption)
- 🐾 1 egg
- 🐾 1 tablespoon coconut oil

Instructions:
1. Preheat oven to 350°F (175°C).
2. Mix all ingredients to form a dough.
3. Roll out and cut into bite-sized pieces.
4. Bake for 15–18 minutes.
5. Cool before serving.

Special Treats for Different Health Needs

Dogs have unique dietary requirements, so their treats should align with their health needs:
- 🐾 **Low-Fat Treats**: Sweet potato chews, banana slices, or homemade dehydrated chicken jerky.
- 🐾 **Grain-Free Options**: Use coconut flour, chickpea flour, or oat flour instead of wheat.
- 🐾 High-Protein Treats: Freeze-dried liver bites, boiled chicken strips, or homemade fish-based treats.
- 🐾 **Hypoallergenic Treats**: Limited-ingredient recipes with single proteins and no common allergens (like wheat or dairy).
- 🐾 **Digestive Health Treats**: Pumpkin-based treats, probiotics in yogurt-based snacks, or fiber-rich apple slices.

How to Prevent Overfeeding Treats

Treats **should be an occasional indulgence** rather than a daily habit, as excessive treat consumption can contribute to weight gain and disrupt a well-balanced diet. To keep treat intake in check, consider offering **smaller portions rather than full-sized treats**. Breaking larger treats into bite-sized pieces allows your dog to enjoy a reward without unnecessary calorie overload. Using treats purposefully, particularly **during training sessions**, ensures they serve as effective motivation rather than just empty snacks. Training treats should be small, flavorful, and given strategically to reinforce positive behaviors rather than being handed out at random.

Regularly monitoring your dog's body condition, energy levels, and overall health can help gauge whether their treat consumption is appropriate. If you notice gradual weight gain or decreased activity, adjusting their treat portions or opting for healthier alternatives like crunchy carrot sticks or apple slices can help maintain a healthy balance. Incorporating nutritious, low-calorie options not only satisfies your dog's craving for snacks but also supports their long-term well-being.

Making homemade treats for your dog allows you to customize their diet and provide nutritious, delicious rewards. Whether your dog needs low-fat, hypoallergenic, or protein-packed snacks, you can tailor recipes to their unique needs. Try out these recipes and watch your dog's tail wag with excitement!

Chapter 11: Feeding Puppies – Special Considerations

Providing proper nutrition during puppyhood is one of the most important steps in ensuring a lifetime of good health. **Puppies grow at an accelerated rate compared to adult dogs**, and their bodies require a well-balanced diet to support bone development, muscle growth, immune function, and brain development. Because of their rapid growth, puppies have **higher energy and nutrient requirements** than adult dogs, making it essential to tailor their meals accordingly.

A homemade diet can provide excellent nourishment for a puppy, but it must be carefully planned to ensure that all their nutritional needs are met at every stage of development. Their diet should contain the right balance of proteins, fats, vitamins, minerals, and carbohydrates to support growth without causing deficiencies or excesses that could lead to health problems later in life.

Preparing Homemade Meals for Puppies

Feeding puppies a homemade diet requires a thoughtful approach, as their growing bodies have specific dietary needs that differ significantly from those of adult dogs. Each meal should be carefully formulated to provide the essential nutrients they require, particularly high-quality proteins, healthy fats, and vital vitamins and minerals.

Protein is the foundation of a puppy's diet, as it fuels muscle growth and overall development. Sources such as chicken, turkey, beef, fish, and eggs provide the necessary amino acids that contribute to strong muscles and tissue repair. Protein should be digestible and lean to prevent excessive weight gain while still supplying the energy required for a growing body.

Healthy fats, particularly omega-3 and omega-6 fatty acids, are crucial for brain development, a shiny coat, and a strong immune system. Puppies benefit greatly from fats found in fish oil, flaxseed oil, and animal-based sources like chicken fat or salmon. These fats support cognitive function, which is especially important during their formative months of training and socialization.

Carbohydrates, while not the primary source of energy for dogs, play a role in maintaining balanced nutrition and providing dietary fiber. Whole grains such as brown rice, quinoa, or oats, along with fiber-rich vegetables like pumpkin, sweet potatoes, and carrots, contribute to digestive health and sustained energy.

Growth Phases and Changing Nutritional Needs

Puppies undergo rapid growth in their first year of life, with different nutritional needs at each stage. Their dietary requirements shift as they transition from newborns to adolescents, necessitating adjustments to portion sizes, nutrient content, and feeding frequency.

During **the first eight weeks**, puppies rely solely on their mother's milk, which provides all the nutrients they need. If a puppy is orphaned or needs supplemental feeding, a specially formulated puppy milk replacer should be used instead of cow's milk, which lacks the necessary nutrients and can cause digestive issues.

At around **four to six weeks of age**, puppies begin the weaning process, where they start transitioning from milk to solid food. This is the ideal time to introduce soft, moistened homemade meals in small portions. Meals should be warm and mushy, resembling a porridge-like consistency that is easy for young teeth to chew. Mixing ground protein sources such as chicken or turkey with a small amount of warm broth and soft vegetables can encourage puppies to explore new textures and flavors.

By eight weeks, most puppies are fully weaned and can eat small, balanced meals multiple times a day. Their diet should be rich in proteins and fats to support rapid development, and meals should be divided into at least four portions per day to accommodate their small stomachs and high energy needs.

Between **three and six months**, puppies experience a growth spurt that requires slightly increased portions, but meal frequency can be gradually reduced to three times a day. At this stage, calcium and phosphorus intake must be closely monitored, particularly in large-breed puppies, to ensure proper bone formation without over-supplementation that could lead to skeletal disorders.

From six months onward, puppies continue growing, but their growth rate begins to slow. Most puppies can transition to twice-a-day feeding, and portion sizes should be adjusted based on their breed size and energy levels. By the time they reach one year of age, small and medium-sized breeds typically complete their growth phase, while large and giant breeds may continue growing until they are 18-24 months old.

Calcium and Phosphorus for Bone Development

Calcium and phosphorus are two of the most vital minerals for a puppy's skeletal health, and their balance is critical for proper bone development. An excess of calcium can lead to abnormal bone growth and joint problems, particularly in large-breed puppies, while a deficiency can result in weak bones and an increased risk of fractures.

The recommended **calcium-to-phosphorus ratio** in a puppy's diet should be approximately **1.2:1**, meaning slightly more calcium than phosphorus. This balance allows bones to develop at the proper rate without growing too quickly, which can put stress on joints.

Best Natural Sources of Calcium and Phosphorus

Certain foods naturally provide the appropriate levels of these minerals. For calcium, **ground eggshells, bone meal**, and dairy products like **plain yogurt** or **cottage cheese** are excellent sources. For phosphorus, animal proteins such as **chicken, beef, and fish** naturally contain high levels of this essential mineral.

Balancing Homemade Meals for Bone Health

While feeding whole bones might seem like a logical way to provide calcium, caution must be exercised. **Raw meaty bones** can be included in raw-fed diets, but cooked bones should never be given, as they can splinter and cause internal injuries. For a safer option, **finely ground bone meal** can be added to homemade puppy meals to ensure they receive the correct amount of calcium.

Large-breed puppies require careful calcium management. Over-supplementing calcium can cause excessive bone growth, leading to painful conditions such as osteochondritis dissecans (OCD) or hip dysplasia. Consulting a veterinarian or canine nutritionist when formulating a homemade diet for a growing large-breed puppy is highly recommended.

Chapter 12 - Homemade Diets for Senior Dogs

As dogs age, their nutritional needs change significantly. Their metabolism slows down, mobility can decline due to joint issues, digestion may become less efficient, and dental health can deteriorate. Adjusting your dog's homemade diet to accommodate these changes is essential for maintaining their quality of life, ensuring they remain active, comfortable, and well-nourished.

Aging dogs require carefully balanced meals that provide the right nutrients without overburdening their digestive system. Unlike younger dogs, seniors often need fewer calories but more targeted nutrition to support their aging bodies. The goal of a senior dog's diet is to maintain a healthy weight, preserve muscle mass, support joint health, and ease digestion while ensuring they receive all the essential vitamins and minerals.

Adjusting Meals for Reduced Metabolism

As dogs enter their senior years, their bodies naturally slow down, and with this change comes a reduced ability to burn calories efficiently. The energy they once used for long walks, playful romps, or even daily movement now accumulates more easily, leading to potential weight gain. This extra weight can put strain on aging joints, making mobility more difficult, and may also place added stress on the heart and other organs. To accommodate this metabolic shift, their diet must be adjusted with careful attention to portion sizes and nutrient balance.

Providing the **right balance of calories without unnecessary excess** requires a thoughtful selection of ingredients. Instead of rich, fatty meats, lean proteins such as turkey, chicken, or white fish become more suitable options, offering the essential nutrients they need without burdening their system with excess fat. These proteins maintain muscle mass, keeping the body strong while reducing the risk of unnecessary weight gain.

To further support a healthy weight, meals should be structured to **promote satiety without excessive caloric intake**. Fiber plays a key role in this, not only aiding digestion but also helping senior dogs feel full and satisfied between meals. Nutrient-dense vegetables such as carrots, pumpkin, and green beans provide bulk and essential vitamins while keeping calorie counts low. These ingredients enhance digestion and contribute to overall well-being by ensuring the body functions smoothly, despite the natural slowing of metabolism.

Rather than serving large meals that may overwhelm the digestive system, **breaking meals into smaller, more frequent portions** allows for steadier energy levels throughout the day. This approach helps regulate blood sugar and prevents the sluggish feeling that can follow a heavy meal. A gentle, consistent feeding routine also ensures that an aging digestive system can process food more efficiently without unnecessary stress.

While fats remain an important part of a senior dog's diet, their intake must be moderated. Excess fats can lead to unhealthy weight gain, making it vital to choose the right sources. Instead of heavy, greasy cuts of meat or large amounts of cooking oils, beneficial fats such as fish oil or flaxseed provide necessary omega-3 fatty acids, supporting skin, coat, and joint health without unnecessary calories. Striking this balance keeps a senior dog nourished, energized, and comfortable as they continue to enjoy their later years.

Supporting Joint and Mobility Health

As dogs age, their once-fluid movements can become slower, and stiffness can begin to set in, often making simple activities like climbing stairs or rising from a nap more challenging. Joint discomfort and arthritis are common in senior dogs, but dietary adjustments can play a significant role in easing pain and improving mobility. By incorporating anti-inflammatory foods and essential joint-supporting nutrients, you can help keep your dog comfortable, active, and engaged in their daily routines.

One of the most powerful tools for joint health is the inclusion of **omega-3 fatty acids**. These beneficial fats, found in sources like fish oil, salmon, sardines, and flaxseed, work to reduce inflammation in aging joints, alleviating pain, and stiffness. By regularly including these nutrient-rich ingredients in meals, dogs may experience improved mobility and a greater willingness to move and play.

Beyond omega-3s, the natural compounds **glucosamine and chondroitin** provide essential support for aging joints. Found in bone broth, chicken cartilage, and green-lipped mussels, these nutrients help maintain cartilage integrity, reducing the deterioration that leads to discomfort. Regular supplementation of these elements can slow the progression of joint issues, offering relief from stiffness and promoting smoother movement.

Turmeric, a golden-hued spice known for its anti-inflammatory properties, is another valuable addition to a senior dog's diet. When paired with a small pinch of black pepper to enhance absorption, turmeric can help ease joint pain, reduce swelling, and support overall mobility. Whether incorporated into meals or blended into homemade treats, this simple addition can provide significant benefits for dogs struggling with arthritis.

Homemade bone broth is a nutritional powerhouse when it comes to joint support. Simmered slowly to extract vital nutrients, it is rich in collagen, glucosamine, and amino acids that work together to promote joint lubrication and flexibility. Offering bone broth as a supplement to meals or as a warming treat on colder days not only supports joint health but also provides hydration and essential nourishment.

To further combat inflammation and support longevity, **meals should be structured around low-carb, nutrient-dense ingredients**. Excess grains and inflammatory foods like white potatoes can contribute to stiffness and sluggishness, making it beneficial to focus on lean proteins and fibrous vegetables instead. Ingredients like leafy greens, carrots, and blueberries provide antioxidants and essential vitamins, reducing oxidative stress while promoting overall wellness.

How to Improve Digestibility

As dogs enter their senior years, their digestive systems may not function as efficiently as they once did. Many older dogs experience slower digestion, reduced enzyme production, and occasional issues like bloating, constipation, or nutrient malabsorption. Because of this, their meals should be tailored to support gut health while remaining easy to process, ensuring they can still absorb all the vital nutrients their bodies need.

One of the most effective ways to aid digestion in senior dogs is by adjusting the way their food is prepared. While raw diets can work well for some dogs, aging digestive systems may struggle with breaking down raw ingredients efficiently. **Lightly cooking proteins and steaming vegetables helps unlock their nutrients**, making them easier to absorb while also reducing the risk of digestive discomfort. Gentle cooking methods preserve the food's natural benefits while making meals more palatable and digestible.

Supporting gut health with **probiotics and prebiotics** is another crucial step in optimizing digestion. A healthy gut microbiome ensures proper nutrient absorption and reduces gastrointestinal issues. Adding natural probiotic sources such as plain Greek yogurt or kefir can introduce beneficial bacteria that help maintain digestive balance. Prebiotic-rich foods like pumpkin or sweet potatoes nourish these good bacteria, promoting a healthier gut environment and reducing issues like constipation or irregular bowel movements.

The type of protein included in meals also plays a role in how easily a senior dog can digest their food. While younger dogs may have no trouble processing red meats like beef or lamb, aging digestive systems can become less efficient at breaking down dense proteins. Switching to lighter, smaller protein molecules found in **white meats like turkey, chicken, or fish** can be gentler on the stomach while still providing essential amino acids. These options are not only easier to digest but also tend to be leaner, helping to maintain a healthy weight.

Hydration is equally important for smooth digestion. Many senior dogs naturally drink less water, which can lead to dehydration and constipation. To combat this, meals should include extra moisture in the form of low-sodium broth, wet food, or water-rich ingredients like cucumbers or zucchini. Increasing fluid intake helps soften food as it moves through the digestive system, making it easier to process and reducing the likelihood of digestive discomfort.

Adjusting Meals for Dental Concerns

As dogs age, dental health becomes a significant factor in their overall well-being. Many senior dogs experience dental issues such as gum disease, worn-down teeth, or even missing teeth, making it painful or difficult to chew hard foods. Adjusting the texture of their meals ensures they can continue to eat comfortably while still receiving the nutrients they need.

One of the most effective ways to **make food more manageable for dogs with dental sensitivities is by softening its texture**. Instead of offering hard kibble, meals can be lightly mashed or pureed, making them easier to chew and swallow. Cooking and shredding proteins, such as chicken or fish, allows them to be eaten with minimal effort, while soft vegetables like sweet potatoes or pumpkin can be blended into a smooth consistency for easy digestion.

Moisture-rich meals provide an excellent alternative to dry food, which can be tough on sensitive teeth and gums. Soaking food in warm bone broth or water helps soften it, making it easier to consume without compromising on nutrition. Lightly stewed meats and slow-cooked vegetables are also great options, as they retain their natural nutrients while offering a gentle texture that aging teeth can handle.

When it comes to treats, senior dogs with dental concerns often struggle with hard biscuits or chews that require excessive gnawing. Instead, opting for **soft treats like banana slices, cooked carrots, or homemade blended snacks** ensures they can still enjoy a reward without discomfort. Rehydrated dog-friendly chews or freeze-dried treats that can be easily softened are also good choices.

Bone broth plays a dual role in supporting dental health. Not only does it help soften meals, but it also provides beneficial nutrients that support gum health and overall immunity. Adding a small amount to meals enhances both flavor and texture, making food more enticing for dogs who may otherwise be reluctant to eat due to oral discomfort.

Conclusion

Providing homemade meals for your dog is one of the most rewarding choices you can make as a pet owner. Not only does it allow you to control the quality of ingredients, but it also strengthens the bond between you and your furry friend. Through this book, you've gained the knowledge to craft balanced, nutritious meals tailored to your dog's unique needs, whether they're a playful puppy, an active adult, or a wise senior.

By now, you understand the importance of proteins, healthy fats, and carbohydrates in your dog's diet, as well as the role of vitamins, minerals, and hydration in keeping them healthy. You've explored how to transition from commercial food to homemade meals, prepare delicious and nutritious treats, and adjust meals for dogs with special dietary needs. With these insights, you're equipped to confidently nourish your dog and support their long-term well-being.

But beyond nutrition, this journey is about love and care. Every meal you prepare is a testament to your dedication to your dog's happiness and health. Watching them thrive on fresh, wholesome food—seeing their coat shine, their energy soar, and their eyes light up with excitement at mealtime—will be the ultimate reward.

As you continue to experiment with recipes, fine-tune portions, and discover your dog's favorite flavors, remember that this is a learning process. Stay flexible, observe your dog's health and behavior, and adjust as needed. And most importantly, enjoy the journey!

Thank you for taking this step toward giving your dog the best possible nutrition. May every bowl you serve be filled with love and may your dog's tail keep wagging for many happy, healthy years to come!

Happy cooking, and even happier tail wags!

Access Your FREE Bonuses

As a special thank-you, I have prepared three exclusive bonuses to help you continue your journey toward better canine nutrition!

Simply scan the QR code to access your free gifts:

Paws Off: Safe and Unsafe Foods for Dogs
A complete guide to human foods that are safe—and those that should always be avoided—to keep your dog happy and healthy.

Bark Bites: Canine Treats for Your Furry Friend
A collection of nutritious, dog-approved treat recipes that are simple to make and perfect for training, rewards, or just because!

Paw-tanical Power: A Natural Supplement Guide for Dogs
Discover the power of natural supplements that can enhance your dog's health, from joint support to digestive wellness, using safe, vet-approved ingredients.

Made in United States
Orlando, FL
06 April 2025